Troy, Michigan

Renee Browning

Contents

Articles

References

Overview of Michigan

Michigan

State of Michigan	

Flag	Seal
Nickname(s): The Great Lakes State, The Wolverine State	
Motto(s): Si quaeris peninsulam amoenam circumspice (If you seek a pleasant peninsula, look about you)	
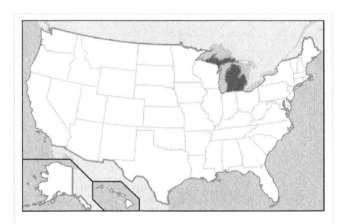	
Official language(s)	None (English, *de-facto*)
Demonym	Michigander Michiganian
Capital	Lansing
Largest city	Detroit
Largest metro area	Metro Detroit
Area	Ranked 11th in the US

- Total	97,990 sq mi (253,793 km^2)
- Width	386 miles (621 km)
- Length	456 miles (734 km)
- % water	41.5
- Latitude	41° 41' N to 48° 18' N
- Longitude	82° 7' W to 90° 25' W
Population	Ranked 8th in the US
- Total	10,045,697 (2008 est.)
- Density	179/sq mi (67.55/km^2) Ranked 16th in the US
- Median income	$44,627 (21st)
Elevation	
- Highest point	Mount Arvon 1,979 ft (603 m)
- Mean	902 ft (275 m)
- Lowest point	Lake Erie 571 ft (174 m)
Admission to Union	January 26, 1837 (26th)
Governor	Jennifer Granholm (D)
Lieutenant Governor	John D. Cherry (D)
Legislature	Michigan Legislature
- Upper house	Senate
- Lower house	House of Representatives
U.S. Senators	• Carl Levin (D) • Debbie Stabenow (D)
U.S. House delegation	8 Democrats 7 Republicans (list)
Time zones	
- most of state	Eastern: UTC-5/-4
- 4 U.P. counties	Central: UTC-6/-5

Abbreviations	MI Mich. US-MI
Website	http://www.michigan.gov

Michigan (^{i} /ˈmɪʃɪgən/) is a U.S. state located in the Great Lakes Region of the United States of America. The name Michigan is a French corruption of the Ojibwe word *mishigama*, meaning "large water" or "large lake".

Michigan is the eighth most populous state in the United States. It has the longest freshwater shoreline of any political subdivision in the world, being bounded by four of the five Great Lakes, plus Lake Saint Clair. In 2005, Michigan ranked third among US states for the number of registered recreational boats, behind California and Florida. Michigan has 64,980 inland lakes and ponds. A person in the state is never more than six miles (10 km) from a natural water source or more than 87.2 miles (140.3 km) from a Great Lakes shoreline. It is the largest state by total area east of the Mississippi River.

Michigan is the only state to consist entirely of two peninsulas. The Lower Peninsula, to which the name Michigan was originally applied, is often dubbed "the mitten" by residents, owing to its shape. The Upper Peninsula (often referred to as "The U.P.") is separated from the Lower Peninsula by the Straits of Mackinac, a five-mile (8 km)-wide channel that joins Lake Huron to Lake Michigan. The Upper Peninsula is economically important for tourism and natural resources.

History

See also: Timeline of Michigan history, History of railroads in Michigan, History of Michigan, and History of Detroit

Michigan was home to Native American cultures before colonization by Europeans. When the first European explorers arrived, the most populous and influential tribes were Algonquian peoples, specifically, the *Ottawa*, the *Anishnabe* (called *Chippewa* in French, after their language *Ojibwe*), and the *Potawatomi*. The Anishnabe, whose numbers are estimated to have been between 25,000 and 35,000, were the most populous.

Although the Anishnabe were well-established in Michigan's Upper Peninsula and northern Lower Peninsula, they also inhabited northern Ontario, northern Wisconsin, southern Manitoba, and northern and north-central Minnesota. The Ottawa lived primarily south of the Straits of Mackinac in northern and western Michigan, while the Potawatomi were primarily in the southwest. The three nations co-existed peacefully as part of a loose confederation called the Council of Three Fires. Other First Nations people in Michigan, in the south and east, were the *Mascouten*, the *Menominee*, the *Miami*, and the Wyandot, who are better known by their French name, *Huron*.

17th century

French *voyageurs*, explored and settled in Michigan in the 17th century. The first Europeans to reach what later became Michigan were those of Étienne Brûlé's expedition in 1622. The first permanent European settlement was founded in 1668 on the site where Father (*Père*, in French) Jacques Marquette established Sault Ste. Marie, Michigan as a Catholic mission to minister to the Ottawa Indians, and to serve as a regional headquarters for further Catholic missionary activities in the upper Great Lakes area. It was here that the first European building was erected in Michigan, within the US Midwest, and also within what is now the Canadian province of Ontario.

Soon afterward, in 1671 the outlying mission of Saint Ignace was founded approximately 50 miles (80 km) south. Then in 1675, French Catholic missionaries founded Marquette approximately 200 miles (320 km) to the west of Sault Ste. Marie, on the south shore of Lake Superior. Together with Sault Ste. Marie, these three original Jesuit missions are the first three European-founded cities in Michigan. Jesuit missionaries were well received by the Indian populations in the area, with relatively few difficulties or hostilities. "The Soo" (Sault Ste. Marie) has the distinction of being the oldest city in both Michigan and Ontario. It was split into two cities in 1818, a year after the U.S.-Canada boundary in the Great Lakes was finally established by the U.S.-U.K. Joint Border Commission following the War of 1812.

In 1679, Lord La Salle of France directed the construction of the *Griffin*, the first European sailing vessel built on the upper Great Lakes. That same year, La Salle built Fort Miami at present-day St. Joseph.

18th century

In 1701, French explorer and army officer Antoine de la Mothe Cadillac founded Le Fort Ponchartrain du Détroit or "Fort Ponchartrain on-the-Strait" on the strait, known as the Detroit River, between lakes Saint Clair and Erie. Cadillac had convinced King Louis XIV's chief minister, Louis Phélypeaux, Comte de Pontchartrain, that a permanent community there would strengthen French control over the upper Great Lakes and repel British aspirations. Cadillac served as the French governor of Louisiana from 1710 to 1716.

Michigan in 1718, Guillaume de L'Isle map, approximate state area highlighted.

The hundred soldiers and workers who accompanied Cadillac built a fort enclosing one arpent (about 0.85 acres (3400 m^2), the equivalent of just under 200 feet (61 m) per side) and named it Fort Pontchartrain. Cadillac's wife, Marie Thérèse Guyon, soon moved to Detroit, becoming one of the first European women to settle in the Michigan wilderness. The town quickly became a major fur-trading and shipping post. The *Église de Saint-Anne* (Church of Saint Ann) was founded the same year. While the original building does not survive, the congregation of that name continues to be active today.

At the same time, the French strengthened Fort Michilimackinac at the Straits of Mackinac to better control their lucrative fur-trading empire. By the mid-18th century, the French also occupied forts at present-day Niles and Sault Ste. Marie, though most of the rest of the region remained unsettled by Europeans.

From 1660 to the end of French rule, Michigan was part of the Royal Province of New France. In 1759, following the Battle of the Plains of Abraham in the French and Indian War (1754–1763), Québec City fell to British forces. This marked Britain's victory in the Seven Years War. Under the 1763 Treaty of Paris, Michigan and the rest of New France east of the Mississippi River passed to Great Britain.

During the American Revolutionary War, Detroit was an important British supply center. Most of the inhabitants were French-Canadians or Native Americans, many of whom had been allied with the French. Because of imprecise cartography and unclear language defining the boundaries in the 1763 Treaty of Paris, the British retained control of Detroit and Michigan after the American Revolution. When Quebec split into Lower and Upper Canada in 1790, Michigan was part of Kent County, Upper Canada. It held its first democratic elections in August 1792 to send delegates to the new provincial parliament at Newark (now Niagara-on-the-Lake).

Under terms negotiated in the 1794 Jay Treaty, Britain withdrew from Detroit and Michilimackinac in 1796. Questions remained over the boundary for many years, and the United States did not have uncontested control of the Upper Peninsula and Drummond Island until 1818 and 1847, respectively.

19th century

During the War of 1812, Michigan Territory (effectively consisting of Detroit and the surrounding area) was captured by the British and nominally returned to Upper Canada. United States forces pushed the British out in 1813 and moved into Canada.

The Treaty of Ghent implemented the policy of *Status Quo Ante Bellum* or "Just as Things Were Before the War." That meant Michigan would remain as part of the United States, and the agreement to establish a joint US-UK boundary commission also remained valid. Subsequent to the findings of that commission in 1817, control of the Upper Peninsula and of islands in the St. Clair River delta was transferred from Ontario to Michigan in 1818. Mackinac Island (to which the British had moved their Michilimackinac army base) was transferred to the U.S. in 1847.

The population grew slowly until the opening of the Erie Canal in New York State 1825 brought a large influx of settlers. Commodities such as grain, lumber, and iron ore could be shipped via the Great Lakes through the Erie Canal and Hudson River. By the 1830s, Michigan had 80,000 residents. More than enough to apply and qualify for statehood. The waterway connection among the Great Lakes states increased the wealth of all.

In October 1835 the people approved the Constitution of 1835, thereby forming a state government, although Congressional recognition was delayed pending resolution of a boundary dispute with Ohio. Both states claimed a 468-square-mile $(1,210\,\text{km}^2)$ strip of land that included the newly incorporated city of Toledo on Lake Erie and an

Lumbering pines in the late 1800s

area to the west then known as the "Great Black Swamp". The dispute came to be called the Toledo War. Michigan and Ohio militia maneuvered in the area but never exchanged fire. Congress awarded the "Toledo Strip" to Ohio. Michigan received the western part of the Upper Peninsula as a concession and formally entered the Union on January 26, 1837.

The Upper Peninsula proved to be a rich source of lumber, iron, and copper. These were among the state's most sought-after natural resources. Geologist Douglass Houghton and land surveyor William Austin Burt were among the first to document many of these resources. Developers rushed to the state. Michigan led the nation in lumber production from 1850s to the 1880s.

The first official meeting of the Republican Party took place July 6, 1854 in Jackson, Michigan, where the party adopted its platform. Michigan made a significant contribution to the Union in the American Civil War and sent more than forty regiments of volunteers to the Federal armies.

Communities and the state rapidly set up systems for public education, including founding the University of Michigan, for a classical academic education, and Ypsilanti Normal College (now Eastern Michigan University, for the training of teachers. Michigan State University in East Lansing was founded as a land-grant college. In the early 20th century, Michigan was the first state to offer a four-year curriculum in a normal college.

20th century to present

See also: History of Ford Motor Company

Michigan's economy underwent a transformation at the turn of the 20th century. The birth of the automotive industry, with Henry Ford's first plant in Highland Park, marked the beginning of a new era in transportation. Like the steamship and railroad, it was a far-reaching development. More than the forms of public transportation, the automobile transformed private life. It became the major industry of Detroit and Michigan, and permanently altered the socio-economic life of the United States and much of the world.

With the growth, the auto industry created jobs in Detroit that attracted immigrants from Europe and migrants from across the country, including both whites and blacks from the rural South. By 1910 Detroit was the fourth largest city in the nation. Residential housing was in short supply, and it took years for the market to catch up with the population boom. By the 1930s, so many immigrants had arrived that more than 30 languages were spoken in the public schools, and ethnic communities celebrated in annual heritage festivals.

Many African Americans moved to Detroit as one of the destinations in the Great Migration from the South, as they could find better work there. Over the years they contributed greatly to its diverse urban culture. African Americans from Detroit created national popular music trends, such as the influential Motown Sound of the 1960s led by a variety of individual singers and groups.

Grand Rapids, the second-largest city in Michigan, is also an important center of manufacturing. Since 1838, the city had also been noted for its thriving furniture industry. Started because of ready sources of lumber, the furniture industry declined in the late 20th century through competition with other regional firms and overseas industry.

Michigan held its first United States presidential primary election in 1910. With its rapid growth in industry, it was an important center of union industry-wide organizing, such as the rise of the United Auto Workers.

In 1920 WWJ in Detroit became the first radio station in the United States to regularly broadcast commercial programs. Throughout that decade, some of the country's largest and most ornate skyscrapers were built in the city. Particularly noteworthy are the Fisher Building, Cadillac Place, and the Guardian Building, each of which is a National Historic Landmarks (NHL).

Detroit boomed through the 1950s, at one point doubling its population in a decade. After World War II, housing development grew outside cities. Newly built highways allowed commuters to navigate the region more easily. In Detroit as elsewhere, many began to move to newer housing in the suburbs.

Michigan is the leading auto-producing state in the U.S., although some of the industry has shifted to less-expensive labor in the Southern United States and overseas. With more than ten million residents, Michigan remains a large and influential state, ranking eighth in population among the fifty states.

The Metro Detroit area in the southeast corner of the state is the largest metropolitan area in Michigan (roughly 50% of the population resides there) and one of the ten largest metropolitan areas in the country. The Grand Rapids/Holland/Muskegon metropolitan area on the west side of the state is the fastest-growing metro area in the state, with over 1.3 million residents as of 2006.

Metro Detroit's population is growing. Detroit's population is stabilizing with a strong redevelopment in the city's central district with a significant rise in population in its outskirts are contributing to some population inflow. A period of economic transition, especially in manufacturing, has caused economic difficulties in the region since the recession of 2001.

Government

See also: List of Governors of Michigan and United States congressional delegations from Michigan

State government

Main article: Government of Michigan

Michigan is governed as a republic, with three branches of government: the executive branch consisting of the Governor of Michigan and the other independently elected constitutional officers; the legislative branch consisting of the House of Representatives and Senate; and the judicial branch consisting of the one court of justice. The state also allows direct participation of the electorate by initiative, referendum, recall, and ratification. Lansing is the state capital and is home to all three branches of state government.

The Governor of Michigan and the other state constitutional officers serve four-year terms and may be re-elected only once. The current Governor is Jennifer Granholm. Michigan has two official Governor's Residences; one is in Lansing, and the other is at Mackinac Island.

The Michigan Legislature consists of a 38-member Senate and 110-member House of Representatives. Senators serve four-year terms and Representatives two. The Michigan State Capitol was dedicated in 1879 and has hosted the state's executive and legislative branches ever since.

Law

The Michigan Court System consists of two courts with primary jurisdiction (the Circuit Courts and the District Courts), one intermediate level appellate court (the Michigan Court of Appeals), and the Michigan Supreme Court. There are several administrative courts and specialized courts. The Michigan Constitution provides for voter initiative and referendum (Article II, § 9, defined as "the power to propose laws and to enact and reject laws, called the initiative, and the power to approve or reject laws enacted by the legislature, called the referendum. The power of initiative extends only to laws which the legislature may enact under this constitution").

In 1846 Michigan was the first state in the Union, as well as the first English-speaking government in the world, to abolish the death penalty. Historian David Chardavoyne has suggested that the movement to abolish capital punishment in Michigan grew as a result of enmity toward the state's neighbor, Canada. Under British rule, it made public executions a regular practice.

Politics

See also: Elections in Michigan and Political party strength in Michigan

Michigan Governor Jennifer
Granholm (D)

Presidential elections results

Year	Republicans	Democrats
2008	40.89% *2,048,639*	**57.33%** *2,872,579*
2004	47.81% *2,313,746*	**51.23%** *2,479,183*
2000	46.14% *1,953,139*	**51.28%** *2,170,418*
1996	38.48% *1,481,212*	**51.69%** *1,989,653*
1992	36.38% *1,554,940*	**43.77%** *1,871,182*
1988	**53.57%** *1,965,486*	45.67% *1,675,783*
1984	**59.23%** *2,251,571*	40.24% *1,529,638*
1980	**48.99%** *1,915,225*	42.50% *1,661,532*
1976	**51.83%** *1,893,742*	46.44% *1,696,714*
1972	**56.20%** *1,961,721*	41.81% *1,459,435*
1968	41.46% *1,370,665*	**48.18%** *1,593,082*
1964	33.10% *1,060,152*	**66.70%** *2,136,615*
1960	48.84% *1,620,428*	**50.85%** *1,687,269*

Voters in the state elect candidates from both major parties. Economic issues are important in Michigan elections. The three-term Republican Governor John Engler (1991–2003) preceded the current

Democratic Governor Jennifer Granholm. The state has re-elected its current Republican Attorney General Mike Cox since 2003. Michigan supported the election of Republican Presidents Ronald Reagan and George H.W. Bush.

However, the state has supported Democrats in the last five presidential election cycles. In 2008, Barack Obama carried the state over John McCain, winning Michigan's seventeen electoral votes with 57% of the vote. Democrats have won each of the last three, nine of the last ten, and fifteen of the last eighteen U.S. Senate elections in Michigan with confidence on national economic issues posing a challenge. Republican strength is greatest in the western, northern, and rural parts of the state, especially in the Grand Rapids area. Republicans also do well in suburban Detroit, which tends to be an important factor in deciding statewide elections. Democrats are strongest in the east, especially in the cities of Detroit, Ann Arbor, Flint, and Saginaw.

Historically, the first formal meeting of the Republican Party took place in Jackson, Michigan on July 6, 1854 and the party thereafter dominated Michigan until the Great Depression. In the 1912 election, Michigan was one of the six states to support progressive Republican and third-party candidate Theodore Roosevelt for President after he lost the Republican nomination to William Howard Taft.

Michigan remained fairly reliably Republican at the presidential level for much of the 20th century. It was part of Greater New England, the northern tier of states settled chiefly by migrants from New England who carried their culture with them. The state was one of only a handful to back Wendell Willkie over Franklin Roosevelt in 1940, and supported Thomas E. Dewey in his losing bid against Harry Truman in 1948. Michigan went to the Democrats in presidential elections during the 1960s, and voted for Republican Richard Nixon in 1972.

Michigan was the home of Gerald Ford, the 38th President of the United States. He was born in Nebraska and moved as an infant to Grand Rapids, Michigan, and grew up there. The Gerald R. Ford Museum is located in Grand Rapids.

Administrative divisions

Main article: Administrative divisions of Michigan

See also: List of Michigan county seats, List of counties in Michigan, and List of municipalities in Michigan (by population)

State government is decentralized among three tiers — statewide, county and township. Counties are administrative divisions of the state, and townships are administrative divisions of a county. Both of them exercise state government authority, localized to meet the particular needs of their jurisdictions, as provided by state law. There are 83 counties in Michigan.

Cities, state universities, and villages are vested with home rule powers of varying degrees. Home rule cities can generally do anything that is not prohibited by law. The fifteen state universities have broad power and can do anything within the parameters of their status as educational institutions that is not prohibited by the state constitution. Villages, by contrast, have limited home rule and are not completely autonomous from the county and township in which they are located.

There are two types of township in Michigan: *general law* township and *charter*. Charter township status was created by the Legislature in 1947 and grants additional powers and stream-lined administration in order to provide greater protection against annexation by a city. As of April 2001, there were 127 charter townships in Michigan. In general, charter townships have many of the same powers as a city but without the same level of obligations. For example, a charter township can have its own fire department, water and sewer department, police department, and so on—just like a city—but it is not *required* to have those things, whereas cities *must* provide those services. Charter townships can opt to use county-wide services instead, such as deputies from the county sheriff's office instead of a home-based force of ordinance officers.

Geography

Further information: Geography of Michigan, Protected areas of Michigan, and List of Michigan state parks

Michigan consists of two peninsulas that lie between 82°30' to about 90°30' west longitude, and are separated by the Straits of Mackinac. The 45th parallel north runs through the state—marked by highway signs and the Polar-Equator Trail—along a line including Mission Point Light near Traverse City, the towns of Gaylord and Alpena and Menominee in the Upper Peninsula. With the exception of two small areas that are drained by the Mississippi River by way of the Wisconsin River in the Upper Peninsula and by way of the Kankakee-Illinois River in the Lower Peninsula, Michigan is drained by the Great Lakes-St. Lawrence watershed and is the only state with the majority of its land thus drained.

The Great Lakes that border Michigan from east to west are Lake Erie, Lake Huron, Lake Michigan and Lake Superior. It has more lighthouses than any other state. The state is bounded on the south by the states of Ohio and Indiana, sharing land and water boundaries with both. Michigan's western boundaries are almost entirely water boundaries, from south to north, with Illinois and Wisconsin in Lake Michigan; then a land boundary with Wisconsin and the Upper Peninsula, that is principally demarcated by the Menominee and Montreal Rivers; then water boundaries again, in Lake Superior, with Wisconsin and Minnesota to the west, capped around by the Canadian province of Ontario to the north and east.

Aerial view of Sleeping Bear Dunes.

Tahquamenon Falls in the Upper Peninsula
of Michigan

The heavily forested Upper Peninsula is relatively mountainous in the west. The Porcupine Mountains, which are part of one of the oldest mountain chains in the world, rise to an altitude of almost 2,000 feet (610 m) above sea level and form the watershed between the streams flowing into Lake Superior and Lake Michigan. The surface on either side of this range is rugged. The state's highest point, in the Huron Mountains northwest of Marquette, is Mount Arvon at 1979 feet (603 m). The peninsula is as large as Connecticut, Delaware, Massachusetts, and Rhode Island combined but has fewer than 330,000 inhabitants. They are sometimes called "Yoopers" (from "U.P.'ers"), and their speech (the "Yooper dialect") has been heavily influenced by the numerous Scandinavian and Canadian immigrants who settled the area during the lumbering and mining boom of the late 19th century.

The Lower Peninsula, shaped like a mitten, is 277 miles (446 km) long from north to south and 195 miles (314 km) from east to west and occupies nearly two-thirds of the state's land area. The surface of the peninsula is generally level, broken by conical hills and glacial moraines usually not more than a few hundred feet tall. It is divided by a low water divide running north and south. The larger portion of the state is on the west of this and gradually slopes toward Lake Michigan. The highest point in the Lower Peninsula is either Briar Hill at 1705 feet (520 m), or one of several points nearby in the

The Pointe Mouillee State Game Area

vicinity of Cadillac. The lowest point is the surface of Lake Erie at 571 feet (174 m).

The geographic orientation of Michigan's peninsulas makes for a long distance between the ends of the state. Ironwood, in the far western Upper Peninsula, lies 630 highway miles (1,015 km) from Lambertville in the Lower Peninsula's southeastern corner. The geographic isolation of the Upper Peninsula from Michigan's political and population centers makes the U.P. culturally and economically distinct. Occasionally U.P. residents have called for secession from Michigan and establishment as a new state to be called "Superior".

A feature of Michigan that gives it the distinct shape of a mitten is the Thumb. This peninsula projects out into Lake Huron and the Saginaw Bay. The geography of the Thumb is mainly flat with a few rolling hills. Other peninsulas of Michigan include the Keweenaw Peninsula, making up the Copper Country region of the state. The Leelanau Peninsula lies in the Northern Lower Michigan region. *See Also Michigan Regions*

Little Sable Point Light south of Pentwater,
Michigan.

Numerous lakes and marshes mark both peninsulas, and the coast is much indented. Keweenaw Bay, Whitefish Bay, and the Big and Little Bays De Noc are the principal indentations on the Upper Peninsula. The Grand and Little Traverse, Thunder, and Saginaw bays indent the Lower Peninsula. Michigan has the ninth longest shoreline of any state—3224 miles (5189 km), including 1056 miles (1699 km) of island shoreline.

The state has numerous large islands, the principal ones being the North Manitou and South Manitou, Beaver, and Fox groups in Lake Michigan; Isle Royale and Grande Isle in Lake Superior; Marquette, Bois Blanc, and Mackinac islands in Lake Huron; and Neebish, Sugar, and Drummond islands in St. Mary's River. Michigan has about 150 lighthouses, the most of any U.S. state. The first lighthouses in Michigan were built between 1818 and 1822. They were built to project light at night and to serve as a landmark during the day to safely guide the passenger ships and freighters traveling the Great Lakes. See Lighthouses in the United States.

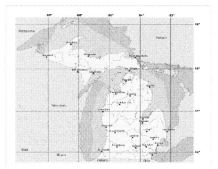

Michigan map, including territorial waters

The state's rivers are generally small, short and shallow, and few are navigable. The principal ones include the Detroit River, St. Marys River, and St. Clair River which connect the Great Lakes; the Au Sable, Cheboygan, and Saginaw, which flow into Lake Huron; the Ontonagon, and Tahquamenon, which flow into Lake Superior; and the St. Joseph, Kalamazoo, Grand, Muskegon, Manistee, and Escanaba, which flow into Lake Michigan. The state has 11,037 inland lakes and 38575 square miles (99910 km^2) of Great Lakes waters and rivers in addition to 1305 square miles (3380 km^2) of inland water. No point in Michigan is more than six miles (10 km) from an inland lake or more than 85 miles (137 km) from one of the Great Lakes.

The state is home to a number of areas maintained by the National Park Service including: Isle Royale National Park, located in Lake Superior, about 30 miles (48 km) southeast of Thunder Bay, Ontario. Other national protected areas in the state include: Keweenaw National Historical Park, Pictured Rocks National Lakeshore, Sleeping Bear Dunes National Lakeshore, Huron National Forest, Manistee National Forest, Hiawatha National Forest, Ottawa National Forest and Father Marquette National Memorial. The largest section of the North Country National Scenic Trail passes through Michigan.

With 78 state parks, 19 state recreation areas, and 6 state forests, Michigan has the largest state park and state forest system of any state. These parks and forests include Holland State Park, Mackinac Island State Park, Au Sable State Forest, and Mackinaw State Forest.

Climate

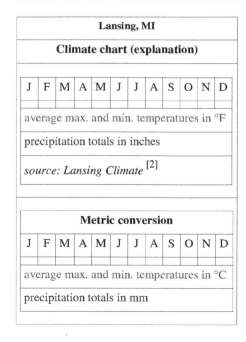

Marquette, MI
Climate chart (explanation)

J	F	M	A	M	J	J	A	S	O	N	D

average max. and min. temperatures in °F

precipitation totals in inches

source: Marquette Climate [3]

Metric conversion

J	F	M	A	M	J	J	A	S	O	N	D

average max. and min. temperatures in °C

precipitation totals in mm

Michigan has a continental climate, although there are two distinct regions. The southern and central parts of the Lower Peninsula (south of Saginaw Bay and from the Grand Rapids area southward) have a warmer climate (Koppen climate classification *Dfa*) with hot summers and cold winters. The northern part of Lower Peninsula and the entire Upper Peninsula has a more severe climate (Koppen *Dfb*), with warm, but shorter summers and longer, cold to very cold winters. Some parts of the state average high temperatures below freezing from December through February, and into early March in the far northern parts. During the winter through the middle of February the state is frequently subjected to heavy lake-effect snow. The state averages from 30–40 inches (76–100 cm) of precipitation annually.

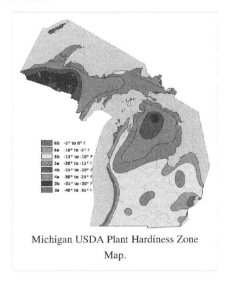

Michigan USDA Plant Hardiness Zone Map.

The entire state averages 30 days of thunderstorm activity per year. These can be severe, especially in the southern part of the state. The state averages 17 tornadoes per year, which are more common in the extreme southern portion of the state. Portions of the southern border have been nearly as vulnerable historically as parts of Tornado Alley. For this reason, many communities in the very southern portions of the state are equipped with tornado sirens to warn residents of approaching tornadoes. Farther north, in the Upper Peninsula, tornadoes are rare.

Monthly Normal High and Low Temperatures For Other Michigan Cities in °F(°C)												
City	Jan	Feb	Mar	Apr	May	Jun	Jul	Aug	Sep	Oct	Nov	Dec
Flint	29/13	32/15	43/24	56/35	69/45	78/55	82/59	80/57	72/49	60/39	46/30	34/19
	(-2/-11)	(0/-9)	(6/-4)	(13/2)	(21/7)	(26/13)	(28/15)	(27/14)	(22/9)	(16/4)	(8/-1)	(1/-7)
Grand Rapids	29/16	33/17	43/26	57/36	70/47	78/56	82/60	80/59	72/51	60/40	46/31	34/21
	(-2/-9)	(1/-8)	(6/-3)	(14/2)	(21/8)	(26/13)	(28/16)	(27/15)	(22/11)	(11/4)	(8/-1)	(1/-6)
Muskegon	30/17	32/18	42/25	55/35	67/45	76/54	80/60	78/59	70/51	59/41	46/32	35/23
	(-1/-8)	(0/-8)	(6/-4)	(13/2)	(19/7)	(24/12)	(27/16)	(26/15)	(21/11)	(15/5)	(8/0)	(2/-5)
Sault Ste. Marie	22/5	24/7	34/16	48/29	63/39	71/46	76/52	74/52	65/45	53/36	39/26	27/13
	(-6/-15)	(-4/-14)	(1/-9)	(9/-2)	(17/4)	(22/7)	(24/11)	(23/11)	(18/7)	(12/2)	(12/-3)	(-3/-11)

[4]

Geology

The geological formation of the state is greatly varied. Primary boulders are found over the entire surface of the Upper Peninsula (being principally of primitive origin), while Secondary deposits cover the entire Lower Peninsula. The Upper Peninsula exhibits Lower Silurian sandstones, limestones, copper and iron bearing rocks, corresponding to the Huronian system of Canada. The central portion of the Lower Peninsula contains coal measures and rocks of the Permo-Carboniferous period. Devonian and sub-Carboniferous deposits are scattered over the entire state.

Demographics

See also: Michigan census statistical areas

n population distribution

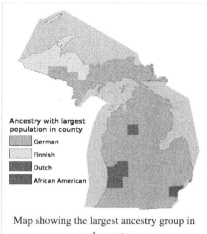

Ancestry with largest
population in county

☐ German

☐ Finnish

☐ Dutch

☐ African American

Map showing the largest ancestry group in
each county

Historical populations		
Census	Pop.	%±
1800	3757	—
1810	4762	26.8%
1820	7452	56.5%
1830	28004	275.8%
1840	212267	658.0%
1850	397654	87.3%
1860	749113	88.4%
1870	1184059	58.1%
1880	1636937	38.2%
1890	2093890	27.9%
1900	2420982	15.6%
1910	2810173	16.1%
1920	3668412	30.5%
1930	4842325	32.0%
1940	5256106	8.5%
1950	6371766	21.2%
1960	7823194	22.8%
1970	8875083	13.4%

1980	9262078		4.4%
1990	9295297		0.4%
2000	9938444		6.9%
Est. 2008	10045697		1.1%

As of July 1, 2008, Michigan had an estimated population of 10,003,422, an increase of 64,930, or 0.7%, since the year 2000. As of 2000, the state had the eighth-largest population in the Union.

The center of population of Michigan is located in Shiawassee County, in the southeastern corner of the civil township of Bennington, which is located directly north of the village of Morrice.

As of 2005-2007 three-year estimate, the state had a foreign-born population of 610,173, or 6% of the total population. In recent years, the foreign-born population in the state has grown. Michigan has the largest Dutch, Finnish, and Macedonian populations in the United States.

As of the 2006-2008 American Community Survey, the racial composition was as follows:

- White: 79.6% (Non-Hispanic Whites: 77.5%)
- Black or African American: 14.0%
- American Indian: 0.5%
- Asian: 2.3%
- Pacific Islander: <0.1%
- Some other race: 1.6%
- Multiracial: 2.0%
- Hispanic or Latino (of any race): 4.0%

Source:

The five largest reported ancestries in Michigan are German (22.4%), African American (14.0%), Irish (12.0%), English (10.6%), and Polish (9.1%).

The large majority of Michigan's population is Caucasian. Americans of European descent live throughout Michigan and most of Metro Detroit. Large European American groups include those of German, Irish, French, and British ancestry. People of Scandinavian descent, especially those of Finnish ancestry, have a notable presence in the Upper Peninsula. Western Michigan is known for the Dutch heritage of many residents (the highest concentration of any state), especially in metropolitan Grand Rapids. Metro Detroit also has residents of Polish and Irish descent.

Dearborn has become the center of a sizeable Arab community, including many Lebanese who immigrated for jobs in the auto industry in the 1920s. About 300,000 people trace their roots to the Middle East which includes. African Americans, who came to Detroit and other northern cities in the Great Migration of the early 20th century, form a majority of the population of the city of Detroit and of other industrial cities, including Flint and Benton Harbor.

An individual from Michigan is called a "Michigander" or "Michiganian". Also at times, but rarely, a "Michiganite". Residents of the Upper Peninsula are sometimes referred to as "Yoopers" (a phonetic pronunciation of "U.P.ers"), and Upper Peninsula residents sometimes refer to those from the lower as "trolls" (they live below the bridge).

					Demographics of Michigan (csv) [5]	
By race	White	Black	AIAN*	Asian	NHPI*
2000 (total population)	83.05%	14.92%	1.26%	2.10%	0.08%
2000 (Hispanic only)	2.98%	0.22%	0.11%	0.03%	0.01%
2005 (total population)	82.65%	15.05%	1.21%	2.57%	0.08%
2005 (Hispanic only)	3.51%	0.23%	0.11%	0.05%	0.02%
Growth 2000–05 (total population)	1.35%	2.77%	-2.51%	24.24%	12.50%
Growth 2000–05 (non-Hispanic only)	0.66%	2.67%	-2.71%	24.04%	10.70%
Growth 2000–05 (Hispanic only)	19.89%	9.70%	-0.48%	36.87%	20.51%
* AIAN is American Indian or Alaskan Native; NHPI is Native Hawaiian or Pacific Islander					

Religion

The Roman Catholic Church was the only organized religion in Michigan until the 19th century, reflecting the territory's French colonial roots. Detroit's St. Anne's parish, established in 1701, is the second-oldest Catholic parish in the country. French-Canadian Catholics were reduced to a small minority by the influx of Protestants from the United States in the early 19th century. By the mid-19th century, there was a wave of immigration of Catholics from Ireland and, later, from eastern and southern Europe.

Change was rapid in the 19th century. The Lutheran Church was introduced by German and Scandinavian immigrants; Lutheranism is second largest religious denomination in the state. The first Jewish synagogue in the state was Temple Beth El, founded by twelve German Jewish families in Detroit in 1850. Islam was introduced by immigrants from the Near East during the 20th century.

The largest denomination by number of adherents, according to a survey in the year 2000, was the Roman Catholic Church with 2,019,926 parishioners. The largest Protestant denominations were the Lutheran Church–Missouri Synod with 244,231 adherents; followed by the United Methodist Church with 222,269; and the Evangelical Lutheran Church in America with 160,836 adherents. In the same survey, Jewish adherents in the state of Michigan were estimated at 110,000, and Muslims at 80,515.

Economy

See also: List of companies based in Michigan and Economy of metropolitan Detroit

The Bureau of Economic Analysis estimated Michigan's 2004 gross state product at $372 B. Per capita personal income in 2003 was $31,178 and ranked twentieth in the nation. In May 2010, the state's seasonally adjusted unemployment rate was 13.6%, with an actual rate of 12.8% for the month, during a U.S. recession.

Top *Fortune* Companies in Michigan for 2009 (ranked by revenues) *with State and U.S. rankings.*		
State	**Corporation**	**US**
1	General Motors	6
2	Ford	7
3	Dow	38
4	Delphi	121
5	Whirlpool	133
6	Ally	147
7	TRW Automotive	169
8	Lear	195
9	Kellogg	210
10	Penske Automotive	225
11	Masco	277
12	Visteon	282
13	DTE Energy	285
14	Arvin Meritor	346
15	CMS Energy	369
16	Stryker	375
17	Autoliv	376
18	Pulte Homes	393
19	Kelly Services	437
20	BorgWarner	453
21	Auto-Owners	476
22	Steelcase	625

23	Borders Group	639
24	Spartan Stores	751
25	Cooper Standard	814
26	Valassis	809
27	Universal Forest	837
28	Affinia Group	853
29	Hayes-Lemmerz	856
30	American Axle	874
31	Herman Miller	897
32	Perrigo	897

Further information:
List of Michigan companies
Source: *Fortune*

Some of the major industries/products/services include automobiles, cereal products, pizza, information technology, aerospace, military equipment, copper, iron, and furniture. Michigan is the third leading grower of Christmas trees with 60520 acres (245 km^2) of land dedicated to Christmas tree farming. The beverage Vernors was invented in Michigan in 1866, sharing the title of oldest soft drink with Hires Root Beer. Faygo was founded in Detroit on November 4, 1907. Two of the top four pizza chains were founded in Michigan and are headquartered there: Domino's Pizza by Tom Monaghan and Little Caesars Pizza by Mike Ilitch.

Michigan has experienced economic difficulties brought on by volatile stock market disruptions following the September 11, 2001 attacks. This caused a pension and benefit fund crisis for many American companies, including General Motors, Ford, and Chrysler. Since the early 2000s recession and the September 11, 2001 attacks, GM, Ford, and Chrysler have struggled to overcome the benefit funds crisis which followed an ensuing volatile stock market which had caused a severe underfunding condition in the respective U.S. pension and benefit funds (OPEB). Although manufacturing in the state grew 6.6% from 2001 to 2006, the high speculative price of oil became a factor for the U.S. auto industry during the economic crisis of 2008 impacting industry revenues.

During this economic crisis, President George W. Bush extended loans from the Troubled Assets Relief Program (TARP) funds in order to help the GM and Chrysler bridge the recession. In January 2009, President Barack Obama formed an automotive task force in order to help the industry recover and achieve renewed prosperity for the region. With retiree health care costs a significant issue, General Motors, Ford, and Chrysler reached agreements with the United Auto Workers Union to transfer the liabilities for their respective health care and benefit funds to a 501(c)(9) Voluntary Employee Beneficiary Association (VEBA). In spite of these efforts, the severity of the recession required

Detroit's automakers to take additional steps to restructure, including idling many plants. With the U.S. Treasury extending the necessary debtor in possession financing, Chrysler and GM filed separate 'pre-packaged' Chapter 11 restructurings in May and June 2009 respectively.

Michigan ranks fourth nationally in high tech employment with 568,000 high tech workers, which includes 70,000 in the automotive industry. Michigan typically ranks third or fourth in overall Research & development (R&D) expenditures in the United States. Its research and development, which includes automotive, comprises a higher percentage of the state's overall gross domestic product than for any other U.S. state. The state is an important source of engineering job opportunities. The domestic auto industry accounts directly and indirectly for one of every ten jobs in the U.S.

Michigan ranked second nationally in new corporate facilities and expansions in 2004. From 1997 to 2004, Michigan was listed as the only state to top the 10,000 mark for the number of major new developments; however, the effects of the late 2000s recession have slowed the state's economy. In 2008, Michigan ranked third in a survey among the states for luring new business which measured capital investment and new job creation per one million population. In August 2009, Michigan and Detroit's auto industry received $1.36 B in grants from the U.S. Department of Energy for the manufacture of electric vehicle technologies which is expected to generate 6,800 immediate jobs and employ 40,000 in the state by 2020. From 2007 to 2009, Michigan ranked 3rd in the U.S. for new corporate facilities and expansions.

As leading research institutions, the University of Michigan, Michigan State University,and Wayne State University are important partners in the state's economy and the state's University Research Corridor. Michigan's public universities attract more than $1.5 B in research and development grants each year. The National Superconducting Cyclotron Laboratory is located at Michigan State University. Michigan's workforce is well-educated and highly skilled, making it attractive to companies. It has the third highest number of engineering graduates nationally.

Detroit Metropolitan Airport is one of the nation's most recently expanded and modernized airports with six major runways, and large aircraft maintenance facilities capable of servicing and repairing a Boeing 747. Michigan's schools and colleges rank among the nation's best. The state has maintained its early commitment to public education. The state's infrastructure gives it a competitive edge; Michigan has 38 deep water ports. In 2007, Bank of America announced that it would commit $25 billion to community development in Michigan following its acquisition of LaSalle Bank in Troy.

Taxation

Michigan's personal income tax is set to a flat rate of 4.35%. Some cities impose additional income taxes. Michigan's state sales tax is 6%. Property taxes are assessed on the local level, but every property owner's local assessment contributes six mills (six dollars per thousand dollars of property value) to the statutory State Education Tax. In 2007, Michigan repealed its Single Business Tax (SBT) and replaced it with a Michigan Business Tax (MBT) in order to stimulate job growth by reducing taxes for seventy percent of the businesses in the state. According to the Bureau of Economic Analysis, recent growth in Michigan is 0.1%.

Agriculture

A wide variety of commodity crops, fruits, and vegetables are grown in Michigan, making it second only to California among U.S. states in the diversity of its agriculture. The state has 55,000 farms utilizing 10000000 acres (40000 km^2) of land which sold $6.6 billion worth of products in 2008. The most valuable agricultural product is milk. Leading crops include corn, soybeans, flowers, wheat, sugar beets and potatoes. Livestock in the state included 1 million cattle, 1 million hogs, 78,000 sheep and over 3 million chickens. Livestock products accounted for 38% of the value of agricultural products while crops accounted for the majority.

Michigan is the leading U.S. producer of tart cherries, blueberries, pickling cucumbers, red beans and petunias.

Michigan is a leading grower of fruit in the U.S., including blueberries, cherries, apples, grapes, and peaches. These fruits are mainly grown in West Michigan. Michigan produces wines, beers and a multitude of processed food products. Kellogg's cereal is based out of Battle Creek, Michigan and processes many locally grown foods. Thornapple Valley, Ballpark Franks, Koegel's, and Hebrew National sausage companies are all based in Michigan.

Michigan is home to very fertile land in the Flint/Tri-Cities and "Thumb" areas. Products grown there include corn, sugar beets, navy beans, and soy beans. Sugar beet harvesting usually begins the first of October. It takes the sugar factories about five months to process the 3.7 million tons of sugarbeets into 970 million pounds of pure, white sugar. Michigan's largest sugar refiner, Michigan Sugar Company is the largest east of the Mississippi River and the fourth largest in the nation. Michigan Sugar brand names are Pioneer Sugar and the newly incorporated Big Chief Sugar. Potatoes are grown in Northern Michigan, and corn is dominant in Central Michigan. Michigan State University is dedicated to the study of agriculture.

Tourism

See also: List of National Historic Landmarks in Michigan, List of Registered Historic Places in Michigan, and List of museums in Michigan

Michigan has a thriving tourist industry. Visitors spend $17.5 billion per year in the state, supporting 193,000 tourism jobs. Michigan's tourism website ranks among the busiest in the nation. Destinations draw vacationers, hunters, and nature enthusiasts from across the United States and Canada. Michigan is fifty percent forest land, much of it quite remote. The forests, lakes and thousands of miles of beaches are top attractions. Event tourism draws large numbers to occasions like the Tulip Time Festival and the National Cherry Festival.

The Grand Hotel on Mackinac Island is a classic image of Michigan tourism.

In 2006, the Michigan State Board of Education mandated that all public schools in the state hold their first day of school after the Labor Day holiday, in accordance with the new Post Labor Day School law. A survey found that 70% of all tourism business comes directly from Michigan residents, and the Michigan Hotel, Motel, & Resort Association claimed that the shorter summer in between school years cut into the annual tourism season in the state.

Tourism in metropolitan Detroit draws visitors to leading attractions, particularly The Henry Ford, the Detroit Institute of Arts, and the Detroit Zoo, and to sports in Detroit. Other museums include the Detroit Historical Museum, the Charles H. Wright Museum of African American History, museums in the Cranbrook Educational Community, and the Arab American National Museum. The metro area offers four major casinos, MGM Grand Detroit, Greektown, Motor City, and Caesars Windsor in Windsor, Ontario, Canada; moreover, Detroit is the largest American city and metropolitan region to offer casino resorts.

Hunting and fishing are significant industries in the state. Charter boats are based in many Great Lakes cities to fish for salmon, trout, walleye and perch. Michigan ranks first in the nation in licensed hunters (over one million) who contribute $2 billion annually to its economy. Over three-quarters of a million hunters participate in white-tailed deer season alone. Many school districts in rural areas of Michigan cancel school on the opening day of firearm deer season, because of attendance concerns.

Michigan's Department of Natural Resources manages the largest dedicated state forest system in the nation. The forest products industry and recreational users contribute $12 billion and 200,000 associated jobs annually to the state's economy. Public hiking and hunting access has also been secured in extensive commercial forests. The state has highest number of golf courses and registered snowmobiles in the nation.

The state has numerous historical markers, which can themselves become the center of a tour. The Great Lakes Circle Tour is a designated scenic road system connecting all of the Great Lakes and the St. Lawrence River.

With its position in relation to the Great Lakes and the countless ships that have foundered over the many years in which they have been used as a transport route for people and bulk cargo, Michigan is a world-class scuba diving destination. The Michigan Underwater Preserves are 11 underwater areas where wrecks are protected for the benefit of sport divers.

Transportation

Michigan has nine international crossings with Ontario, Canada:

Mackinac Bridge

- Ambassador Bridge, North America's busiest international border crossing the Detroit River
- Blue Water Bridge, a twin-span bridge (Port Huron, Michigan and Point Edward, Ontario, but the larger city of Sarnia, Ontario is usually referred to on the Canadian side.)
- Blue Water Ferry (Marine City, Michigan and Sombra, Ontario)
- Canadian Pacific Railway tunnel.
- Detroit–Windsor Truck Ferry (Detroit, Michigan and Windsor, Ontario)
- Detroit–Windsor Tunnel.
- International Bridge (Sault Ste. Marie, Michigan and Sault Ste. Marie, Ontario)
- St. Clair River Railway Tunnel (Port Huron, Michigan and Sarnia, Ontario)
- Walpole Island Ferry (Algonac, Michigan and Walpole Island First Nation, Ontario

A second international bridge is currently under development between Detroit, Michigan and Windsor, Ontario.

Railroads

See also: List of Michigan railroads and History of railroads in Michigan

Michigan is served by four Class I railroads: the Canadian National Railway, the Canadian Pacific Railway, CSX Transportation, and the Norfolk Southern Railway. These are augmented by several dozen short line railroads. The vast majority of rail service in Michigan is devoted to freight, with Amtrak and various scenic railroads the exceptions.

Main article: Michigan Services

Amtrak passenger rail services the state, connecting many southern and western Michigan cities to Chicago, Illinois. There are plans for commuter rail for Detroit and its suburbs (see SEMCOG Commuter Rail).

Roadways

See also: Michigan Highway System

Interstate 75 is the main thoroughfare between Detroit, Flint, and Saginaw extending north to Sault Sainte Marie and providing access to Sault Sainte Marie, Ontario. The expressway crosses the Mackinac Bridge between the Lower and Upper Peninsulas. Branching highways include I-275 and I-375 in Detroit; I-475 in Flint; and I-675 in Saginaw.

Welcome sign.

Interstate 69 enters the state near the Michigan-Ohio-Indiana border, and it extends to Port Huron and provides access to the Blue Water Bridge crossing into Sarnia, Ontario.

Interstate 94 enters the western end of the state at the Indiana border, and it travels east to Detroit and then northeast to Port Huron and ties in with I-69. I-194 branches off from this freeway in Battle Creek. I-94 is the main artery between Chicago, Illinois and Detroit.

Interstate 96 runs east–west between Detroit and Muskegon. I-496 loops through Lansing. I-196 branches off from this freeway at Grand Rapids and connects to I-94 near Benton Harbor. I-696 branches off from this freeway at Novi and connects to I-94 near St Clair Shores.

U.S. Route 2 enters Michigan at the city of Ironwood and runs east to the town of Crystal Falls, where it turns south and briefly re-enters Wisconsin northwest of Florence. It re-enters Michigan north of Iron Mountain and continues through the Upper Peninsula of Michigan to the cities of Escanaba, Manistique, and St. Ignace. Along the way, it cuts through the Ottawa and Hiawatha National Forests and follows the northern shore of Lake Michigan. Its eastern terminus lies at exit 344 of I-75, just north of the Mackinac Bridge. This is generally regarded as the main route through the Upper Peninsula, although some prefer to travel on M-28 as it tends to save time (U.S. 2 hugs the Lake Michigan shoreline for much of its length.)

Major bridges include the Ambassador Bridge, Blue Water Bridge, Mackinac Bridge, and International Bridge. Michigan also has the Detroit-Windsor Tunnel crossing into Canada.

Airports

See also: List of airports in Michigan

The Detroit Metropolitan Wayne County Airport is Michigan's busiest airport, followed by the Gerald R. Ford International Airport in Grand Rapids.

Important cities and townships

Further information: List of cities, villages, and townships in Michigan

The largest municipalities in Michigan are (according to 2009 census estimates):

The Grand Rapids skyline centered on the Grand River.

A Lansing sunset

Downtown Flint as seen from the Flint River.

The Ann Arbor skyline as seen from Michigan Stadium.

Rank	City	Population	Image
1	Detroit	910,920	
2	Grand Rapids	193,710	
3	Warren	133,872	
4	Sterling Heights	127,176	
5	Lansing	113,810	
6	Ann Arbor	112,852	
7	Flint	111,475	
8	Clinton Township	95,990	
9	Livonia	89,282	Map showing largest Michigan municipalities.
10	Dearborn	84,575	

Other important cities include:

- Battle Creek ("Cereal City U.S.A.", world headquarters of Kellogg Company)
- Benton Harbor / St. Joseph (headquarters of Whirlpool Corporation)
- East Lansing (home of Michigan State University)
- Big Rapids (home of Ferris State University)
- Holland (home of Tulip Time, the largest tulip festival in the U.S.)
- Jackson (headquarters of CMS Energy)
- Kalamazoo (Largest city in southwest Michigan and home to Western Michigan University)
- Manistee (home to the world's largest salt plant, owned by Morton Salt)
- Marquette (largest city in the Upper Peninsula with 19,661 people and home of Northern Michigan University)
- Midland (headquarters of the Dow Chemical Company and the Dow Corning Corporation)
- Mount Pleasant (home of Central Michigan University)
- Muskegon (largest Michigan city on Lake Michigan)
- Pontiac (major automobile manufacturing center, and home of the Pontiac Silverdome)
- Port Huron (major international crossing and home of the Blue Water Bridge)
- Saginaw (the largest of the Tri-Cities, which also consist of Bay City and Midland, and home to Saginaw Valley State University)
- Sault Ste. Marie (home of the Soo Locks and Sault Ste. Marie International Bridge)
- Traverse City ("Cherry Capital of the World", making Michigan the country's largest producer of cherries)
- Ypsilanti (home of Eastern Michigan University)

Half of the wealthiest communities in the state are located in Oakland County, just north of Detroit. Another wealthy community is located just east of the city, in Grosse Pointe. Only three of these cities are located outside of Metro Detroit. The city of Detroit itself, with a per capita income of $14,717, ranks 517th on the list of Michigan locations by per capita income. Benton Harbor is the poorest city in Michigan, with a per capita income of $8,965, while Barton Hills is the richest with a per capita income of $110,683.

Education

See also: List of colleges and universities in Michigan and List of high schools in Michigan

Michigan's education system provides services to 1.6 million K-12 students in public schools. More than 124,000 students attend private schools and an uncounted number are homeschooled under certain legal requirements. The public school system has a $14.5 billion budget in 2008-2009. Michigan has a number of public universities spread throughout the state and a numerous private colleges as well. Michigan State University has one of the largest enrollments of any U.S. school. Michigan State and University of Michigan are leading research institutions.

Professional sports

Main article: List of Michigan professional sports teams

Michigan's major-league sports teams include: Detroit Tigers baseball team, Detroit Lions football team, Detroit Red Wings ice hockey team, and the Detroit Pistons men's basketball team.

The Pistons played at Detroit's Cobo Arena until 1978 and at the Pontiac Silverdome until 1988 when they moved into the Palace of Auburn Hills. The Detroit Lions played at Tiger Stadium in Detroit until 1974, then moved to the Pontiac Silverdome where they played for 27 years between 1975-2002 before moving to Ford Field in Detroit in 2002. The Detroit Tigers played at Tiger Stadium (Detroit) (formerly known as Navin Field and Briggs Stadium) from 1912 to 1999. In 2000 they moved to Comerica Park. The Red Wings played at Olympia Stadium before moving to Joe Louis Arena in 1979.

Thirteen-time Grand Slam champion Serena Williams was born in Saginaw. The Michigan International Speedway is the site of NASCAR races and Detroit was formerly the site of a Grand Prix race. Michigan is home to one of the major canoeing marathons: the 120-mile (190 km) Au Sable River Canoe Marathon. Professional hockey got its start in Houghton, when the Portage Lakers were formed.

State symbols and nicknames

Michigan is, by tradition, known as "The Wolverine State," and the University of Michigan takes the wolverine as its mascot. The association is well and long established: for example, many Detroiters volunteered to fight during the American Civil War and George Armstrong Custer, who led the Michigan Brigade, called them the "Wolverines". The origins of this association are obscure; it may derive from a busy trade in wolverine furs in Sault Ste. Marie in the 18th century or may recall a disparagement intended to compare early settlers in Michigan with the vicious mammal. Wolverines are, however, extremely rare in Michigan. A sighting in February 2004 near Ubly was the first confirmed sighting in Michigan in 200 years. The animal was found dead in 2010.

- State nicknames: *Wolverine State*, *Great Lakes State*, *Mitten State*, *Water-Winter Wonderland*
- State motto: *Si quaeris peninsulam amoenam circumspice* (Latin: If you seek a pleasant peninsula, look about you) adopted in 1835 on the coat-of-arms, but never as an official 'motto'. This is a paraphrase of the epitaph of British architect Sir Christopher Wren about his masterpiece, St. Paul's Cathedral.
- State song: *My Michigan* (official since 1937, but disputed amongst residents), *Michigan, My Michigan* (Unofficial State Song, since the civil war)
- State bird: American Robin (since 1931)
- State animal: Wolverine (traditional)
- State game animal: White-tailed deer (since 1997)
- State fish: Brook trout (since 1965)
- State reptile: Painted Turtle (since 1995)
- State fossil: Mastodon (since 2000)
- State flower: Apple blossom (adopted in 1897, official in 1997)
- State wildflower: Dwarf Lake Iris (since 1998). Known as *Iris lacustris*, it is a federally listed threatened species.
- State tree: White pine (since 1955)
- State stone: Petoskey stone (since 1965). It is composed of fossilized coral (*Hexagonaria pericarnata*) from long ago when the middle of the continent was covered with a shallow sea.
- State gem: Isle Royale greenstone (since 1973). Also called *chlorastrolite* (literally "green star stone"), the mineral is found on Isle Royale and the Keweenaw peninsula.
- State Quarter: U.S. coin issued in 2004 with the Michigan motto "Great Lake State."
- State soil: Kalkaska Sand (since 1990), ranges in color from black to yellowish brown, covers nearly 1000000-acre (4000 km^2) in 29 counties.

Sister states

- Shiga Prefecture, Japan
- Sichuan Province, Peoples Republic of China

See also

- Outline of Michigan
- Index of Michigan-related articles
- USS Michigan

Further reading

- Bald, F. Clever, *Michigan in Four Centuries* (1961)/
- Browne, William P. and - Kenneth VerBurg. *Michigan Politics & Government: Facing Change in a Complex State* University of Nebraska Press. 1995.
- Bureau of Business Research, Wayne State U. *Michigan Statistical Abstract* (1987).
- Clarke Historical Library, Central Michigan University, Bibliographies for Michigan by region, counties, etc. [6].
- Dunbar, Willis F. and George S. May. *Michigan: A History of the Wolverine State* (1995) excerpt and text search [7]
- Michigan, State of. *Michigan Manual* (annual), elaborate detail on state government.
- Press, Charles et al., *Michigan Political Atlas* (1984).
- Public Sector Consultants. *Michigan in Brief. An Issues Handbook* (annual)
- Rich, Wilbur. *Coleman Young and Detroit Politics: From Social Activist to Power Broker* (Wayne State University Press, 1988).
- Rubenstein, Bruce A. and Lawrence E. Ziewacz. *Michigan: A History of the Great Lakes State.* (2nd ed. 2008)
- Sisson, Richard, Ed. *The American Midwest: An Interpretive Encyclopedia* (2006)
- Weeks, George, *Stewards of the State: The Governors of Michigan* (Historical Society of Michigan, 1987).

External links

- State of Michigan government website [8]
- Energy Data & Statistics for Michigan [9]
- Info Michigan, detailed information on 630 cities [10]
- Michigan Historic Markers [11]
- Michigan History Magazine [12]
- Michigan Lighthouse Chronology - Clark Historical Library [13]
- Michigan State Guide from the Library of Congress [14]
- Michigan Official Travel Site [15]
- Michigan travel guide from Wikitravel
- Michigan [16] at the Open Directory Project
- Michigan State Fact Sheet [17] from the U.S. Department of Agriculture
- Michigan Underwater Preserves Council [18]
- The Michigan Municipal League [19]
- USGS real-time, geographic, and other scientific resources of Michigan [20]

Bold Faced States/Provinces bound Michigan completely over water.

Bold Italicized States bound Michigan partially over water.

None of Michigan's neighbors border them completely over land. Even Indiana and Ohio have small portions of border that is over one of the Great Lakes, Lake Michigan (Indiana) and Lake Erie (Ohio).

Wisconsin's border with Michigan is mainly over water except for most of their border with the Upper Peninsula, which is over land and to the southwest.

1. REDIRECT Template:Navboxes

Geographical coordinates: 44°20′N 85°35′W

frr:Michigan pnb:مشیگن

History of Michigan

The **History of Michigan** is divided into the following articles.

See also Timeline of Michigan history.

Main article: Michigan

Aerial photo of Soo Locks and International Bridge displaying the historic relationships Michigan has with the Great Lakes and Canada.

Before 1776

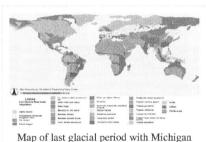

Map of last glacial period with Michigan and Great Lakes Basin entirely covered by an ice sheet.

Thousands of years before the arrival of the first Europeans, several indigenous tribes lived in what is today the state of Michigan. They included the Ojibwa, Menominee, Miami, Ottawa, and Potawatomi, who were part of the Algonquian family of Amerindians, as well as the Wyandot, who were from the Iroquoian family and lived in the area of present-day Detroit. It is estimated that the native population at the time the first European arrived was 15,000.

The first white explorer to visit Michigan was the Frenchman Étienne Brûlé in 1620, who began his expedition from Quebec City on the orders of Samuel de Champlain and traveled as far as the Upper Peninsula. Afterward, the area became part of Louisiana, one of the large colonial provinces of New France. The first permanent European settlement in Michigan was founded in 1668 at Sault Ste. Marie by Jacques Marquette, a French missionary.

The French built several trading posts, forts, and villages in Michigan during the late 17th century. Among them, the most important was Fort Pontchartrain du Détroit, established by Antoine de Lamothe Cadillac. This grew to become Detroit. Up until this time, French activities in the region were limited to hunting, trapping, trading with and the conversion of local Indians, and some limited

Michigan in 1718, Guillaume de L'Isle map, approximate state area highlighted.

subsistence agriculture. By 1760, the Michigan countryside had only a few hundred white inhabitants.

Territorial disputes between French and British colonists helped start the French and Indian War as part of the larger Seven Years' War, which took place from 1754 to 1763 and resulted in the defeat of France. As part of the Treaty of Paris, the French ceded all of their North American colonies east of the Mississippi River to Britain. Thus the future Michigan was handed over to the British. In 1774, the area was made part of Quebec. It continued to be sparsely populated. Regional growth proceeded slowly because the British were more interested in the fur trade and peace with the natives than in settlement of the area.

From 1776 to 1837

During the American Revolutionary War, the local European population, who were primarily American colonists that supported independence, rebelled against Britain. The British, with the help of local tribes, continually attacked American settlements in the region starting in 1776 and conquered Detroit. In 1781, Spanish raiders led by a French Captain Eugene Poure travelled by river and overland from St Louis, liberated British-held Fort St Joseph, and handed authority over the settlement to the Americans the following day. The war ended with the signing of the Treaty of Paris in 1783, and Michigan passed into the control of the newly formed United States of America. In 1787, the region became part of the Northwest Territory. The British, however, continued to occupy Detroit and other fortifications and did not definitively

Unfinished contemporaneous painting of the American diplomatic negotiators of the Treaty of Paris which brought official conclusion to the Revolutionary War and gave possession of Michigan and other territory to the new United States.

leave the area until after the implementation of the Jay Treaty in 1796.

The land which is now Michigan was made part of Indiana Territory in 1800. Most was declared as Michigan Territory in 1805, including all of the Lower Peninsula. During the War of 1812, British forces from Canada captured Detroit and Fort Mackinac early on, giving them a strategic advantage and encouraging native revolt against the United States. American troops retook Detroit in 1813 and Fort Mackinac was returned to the Americans at the end of the war in 1815.

Over the 1810s, the indigenous Ojibwa, Ottawa, and Potawatomi tribes increasingly decided to oppose white settlement and sided with the British against the U.S. government.

After their defeat in the War of 1812, the tribes were forced to sell all of their land claims to the US federal government by the Treaty of Saginaw and the Treaty of Chicago. After the war, the government built forts in some of the northwest territory, such as at Sault Ste. Marie. In the 1820s the US government assigned Indian agents to work with the tribes, including arranging land cessions and relocation. They forced most of the Native Americans to relocate from Michigan to Indian reservations further west.

During the 1820s, the population of Michigan Territory grew rapidly, largely because of the opening of the Erie Canal in 1825. Its connection of the navigable waters of the middle Great Lakes to those of the Atlantic Ocean dramatically sped up transportation between the eastern states and the less-inhabited western territories. The canal created new possibilities for transport of produce and goods to market, as well as easing passage of migrants to the west.

Michigan's oldest university, the University of Michigan was founded in Detroit in 1817 and was later moved to its present location in Ann Arbor. The state's oldest cultural instititon, the Historical Society of Michigan, was established by territorial governor Lewis Cass and explorer Henry Schoolcraft in 1828.

Rising settlement prompted the elevation of Michigan Territory to that of the present-day state. In 1835, the federal government enacted a law that would have created a State of Michigan. A territorial dispute with Ohio over the Toledo Strip, a stretch of land including the city of Toledo, delayed the final accession of statehood. The disputed zone became part of Ohio by the order of a revised bill passed by the U.S. Congress and signed into law by President Andrew Jackson which also gave compensation to Michigan in the form of control of the Upper Peninsula. On January 26, 1837, Michigan became the 26th state of the Union.

From 1837 to 1900

During the early 1840s, large deposits of copper and iron ores were discovered on the Upper Peninsula.

Michigan actively participated in the American Civil War sending thousands of volunteers. After the war, the local economy became more varied and began to prosper economically. During the 1870s, the lumber industry, dairy farming and diversified industry grew rapidly in the state. The population doubled between 1870 and 1890.

Toward the end of the century, the state government established a state school system on the German model, with public schools, high schools, normal schools or colleges for training teachers of lower grades, and colleges for classical academic studies and professors. It dedicated more funds to public education than did any other state in the nation. Within a few years, it established four-year curriculums at its normal colleges, and was the first state to establish a full college program for them.

Railroads have been vital in the history of the population and trade of rough and finished goods in the state of Michigan. While some coastal settlements had previously existed, the population, commercial, and industrial growth of the state further bloomed with the establishment of the railroad.

1900 to 1941

During the early 20th century, manufacturing industries became the main source of revenue for Michigan – in large part, because of the automobile. In 1899, the Olds Motor Vehicle Company opened a factory in Detroit. In 1903, Ford Motor Company was also founded there. With the mass production of the Ford Model T, Detroit became the world capital of the auto industry. General Motors is based in Detroit, Chrysler is located in Rochester Hills, and Ford is headquartered in nearby Dearborn. Both corporations constructed large industrial complexes in the Detroit metropolitan area, exemplified by the River Rouge Plant, which have made Michigan a national leader in manufacturing since the 1910s. This industrial base produced greatly during World War I, filling a huge demand for military vehicles.

Photo of workers occupying a General Motors car body factory during the Flint Sit-Down Strike which spurred the organization of unions in the U.S. auto industry.

Jackson was home to one of the first car industry developments. Even before Detroit began building cars on assembly lines, Jackson was busy making parts for cars and putting them together in 1901. By 1910, the auto industry became Jackson's main industry. Over twenty different cars were once made in Jackson. Including: Reeves, Jaxon, Jackson, CarterCar, Orlo, Whiting, Butcher and Gage, Buick, Janney, Globe, Steel Swallow, C.V.I., Imperial, Ames-Dean, Cutting, Standard Electric, Duck, Briscoe, Argo, Hollier, Hackett, Marion-Handly, Gem, Earl, Wolverine, and Kaiser-Darrin. Today the auto industry remains one of the largest employers of skilled machine operators in Jackson County.

With the expansion of industry, hundreds of thousands of migrants from the South and immigrants from eastern and southern Europe were attracted to Detroit. In a short time, it became the fourth largest city in the country - housing shortages persisted for years even as new housing was developed throughout the city. Ethnic immigrant enclaves rapidly developed where churches, bakeries and businesses supported unique communities. A guide to the city written in the 1930s noted that there were students speaking more than 35 languages in the public schools. Ethnic festivals were a regular part of the city's culture. At the same time, such rapid social change created an environment in which the second Ku Klux Klan recruited members in the city. Their influence was at a peak in 1925, but membership fell quickly after that.

The Great Depression caused severe economic hardship in Michigan. Thousands of auto industry workers were dismissed along with other workers from several sectors of the state economy. The financial suffering was aggravated by the fact that remaining copper reserves in the state lay deep underground. With the discovery of copper finds in other states located in less deep rock layers, local mining fell sharply and resulted in unemployment for thousands of miners. The federal government took several measures to try to diminish the negative effects. It created the Civilian Conservation Corps, a work relief program that started hiring thousands of unemployed young men for jobs like maintenance and cleaning. The Works Progress Administration was another federal agency which hired more than 500,000 unemployed people in Michigan alone to construct major public works such as roads, buildings, and dams.

During this time, United Auto Workers was founded to represent automotive industry employees. This labor union pressured Michigan auto companies to hire for contract only workers who were union members and wanted to handle negotiations between managers and workers. Ford and General Motors became the main targets of the UAW, and continuous strikes, the most important of which was the Flint Sit-Down Strike, forced both companies to recognize the existence of the union. Today, the UAW is one of the largest unions in the United States and has represented all of the employed workers of domestic automobile companies since 1941.

After 1941

The entry of the United States into World War II the same year ended the economic contraction in Michigan. Wartime required the large-scale production of weapons and military vehicles, leading to a massive number of new jobs being filled. After the end of the war, both the automotive and copper mining industries recovered.

Starting during WWI, the Great Migration fueled the movement of thousands of African-Americans from the South to industrial jobs in Michigan and, especially, Detroit. Migration of white southerners to the city increased the volatility of change. Population increases continued with industrial expansion during WWII and afterward. African Americans contributed to a new vibrant urban culture, with expansion of new music, food and culture.

The postwar years were initially a prosperous time for industrial workers, who achieved middle-class livelihoods. These were the years of the creation and popularity of Motown Records. By late mid-century, however, deindustrialization and restructuring cost many jobs. The economy suffered and the city postponed needed changes. Neglect of social problems and urban decline fed racial conflicts. In 1967 the 12th St. Riot erupted, lasting eight days, causing 25 million dollars in damages, and resulting in 43 deaths. The violence caused many people to leave the city who could, to avoid future problems.

Gerald Ford, a politician from Grand Rapids who was elected to the House of Representatives thirteen times and also served as House Minority Leader and then Vice President, became the 38th President of the United States after the resignation of Richard Nixon.

The 1973 Oil Crisis caused economic recession in the United States and greatly affected the Michigan economy. Afterward, automobile companies in the United States faced greater multinational competition, especially from Japan. As a consequence, domestic auto makers enacted cost-cutting measures to remain competitive at home and abroad. Unemployment rates rose dramatically in the state.

Throughout the 1970s, Michigan possessed the highest unemployment rate of any U.S. state. Large spending cuts to education and public health were repeatedly made in an attempt to reduce growing state budget deficits. A strengthening of the auto industry and an increase in tax revenue stabilized government and household finances in the 1980s. Increasing competition by Japanese and South

Korean auto companies continues to challenge the state economy, which depends heavily on the automobile industry. Since the late 1980s, the government of Michigan has actively sought to attract new industries, thus reducing economic reliance on a single sector.

Further reading

- Bald, F. Clever, *Michigan in Four Centuries* (1961)/
- Browne, William P. and - Kenneth VerBurg. *Michigan Politics & Government: Facing Change in a Complex State* University of Nebraska Press. 1995.
- Bureau of Business Research, Wayne State U. *Michigan Statistical Abstract* (1987).
- Clarke Historical Library, Central Michigan University, Bibliographies for Michigan by region, counties, etc. [6].
- Dunbar, Willis F. and George S. May. *Michigan: A History of the Wolverine State* (1995) excerpt and text search [7]
- Michigan, State of. *Michigan Manual* (annual), elaborate detail on state government.
- *Michigan Historical Review* Central Michigan University (quarterly).
- Nolan, Alan T. *The Iron Brigade: A Military History* (1994), famous Civil War combat unit
- Press, Charles et al., *Michigan Political Atlas* (1984).
- Public Sector Consultants. *Michigan in Brief. An Issues Handbook* (annual)
- Rich, Wilbur. *Coleman Young and Detroit Politics: From Social Activist to Power Broker* (Wayne State University Press, 1988).
- Rubenstein, Bruce A. and Lawrence E. Ziewacz. *Michigan: A History of the Great Lakes State.* (2002)
- Sisson, Richard, Ed. *The American Midwest: An Interpretive Encyclopedia* (2006)
- Trap. Paul, and Larry Wagenaar. *Michigan History Directory of Historical Societies, Museums, Archives, Historic Sites, Agencies and Commissions* (12th Ed. 2008)
- Weeks, George, *Stewards of the State: The Governors of Michigan* (Historical Society of Michigan, 1987).

See also

Main article: Historical outline of Michigan

- Algonquian peoples
- European colonization of the Americas
- History of Detroit
- History of Ford Motor Company
- History of General Motors
- History of railroads in Michigan
- History of the Midwestern United States
- International Boundary Waters Treaty
- Inland Northern American English

- Northwest Ordinance
- List of Michigan county name etymologies
- List of museums in Michigan
- Sixty Years' War
- Timeline of Michigan history
- Timeline of the Toledo Strip/War
- War of 1812

External links

- Historical Society of Michigan [1]
- Official State of Michigan History, Arts & Libraries homepage (MHAL) [2]

Geography of Michigan

Michigan consists of two peninsulas that lie between 82°30' to about 90°30' west longitude, and are separated by the Straits of Mackinac, and some nearby islands. With the exception of two small areas that are drained by the Mississippi River by way of the Wisconsin River in the Upper Peninsula and by way of the Kankakee-Illinois River in the Lower Peninsula, Michigan is drained by the Great Lakes-St. Lawrence watershed and is the only state with the majority of its land thus drained.

Michigan map, including territorial waters.

Great Lakes

The Great Lakes that border Michigan from east to west are Lake Erie, Lake Huron, Lake Michigan and Lake Superior. Because of the lakes, Michigan has more lighthouses than any other state.[citation needed] The state is bounded on the south by the states of Ohio and Indiana, sharing land and water boundaries with both. Michigan's western boundaries are almost entirely water boundaries, from south to north, with Illinois and Wisconsin in Lake

Michigan; then a land boundary with Wisconsin and the Upper Peninsula, that is principally demarcated by the Menominee and Montreal Rivers; then water boundaries again, in Lake Superior, with Wisconsin and Minnesota to the west, capped around by the Canadian province of Ontario to the north and east.

The northern boundary then runs completely through Lake Superior, from the western boundary with Minnesota to a point north of and around Isle Royale, thence traveling southeastward through the lake in a reasonably straight line to the Sault Ste. Marie area. In Southeastern Michigan there is a water boundary with Canada along the entire lengths of the St. Clair River, Lake St. Clair (including the First Nation reserve of Walpole Island) and the Detroit River). The southeastern boundary ends in the western end of Lake Erie with a three-way convergence of Michigan, Ohio and Ontario.

Aerial View of Sleeping Bear Dunes

The Pointe Mouillee State Game Area

Tahquamenon Falls in the Upper Peninsula of Michigan.

Michigan encompasses 58,110 square miles (150,504 km²) of land, 38,575 square miles (99,909 km²) of Great Lakes waters and 1,305 square miles (3,380 km²) of inland waters. Only Alaska has more territorial water. At a total of 97,990 square miles (253,793 km²), Michigan is the largest state east of the Mississippi River (inclusive of its territorial waters). Michigan claims a land area of 58110 square miles (150500 km^2) of land and 97990 sq mi (253790 km^2) total, making it the tenth largest state, but the U.S. Census Bureau claims only 56803.82 sq mi (147121.22 km^2) of land and 96716.11 sq mi (250493.57 km^2) total, making it the eleventh largest. Michigan forestland covers nearly 52% of the state at 19300000 acres (78000 km^2).

Upper Peninsula

The heavily forested Upper Peninsula is relatively mountainous in the west. The Porcupine Mountains, which are part of one of the oldest mountain chains in the world, rise to an altitude of almost 2,000 feet (610 m) above sea level and form the watershed between the streams flowing into Lake Superior and Lake Michigan. The surface on either side of this range is rugged. The state's highest point, in the Huron Mountains northwest of Marquette, is Mount Arvon at 1,979 feet (603 m). The peninsula is as large as Connecticut, Delaware, Massachusetts, and Rhode Island combined but has fewer than 330,000 inhabitants. They are sometimes called "Yoopers" (from "U.P.'ers"), and their speech (the "Yooper dialect") has been heavily influenced by the numerous Scandinavian and Canadian immigrants who settled the area during the lumbering and mining boom of the late nineteenth century.

The geographic orientation of Michigan's peninsulas makes for a long distance between the ends of the state. Ironwood, in the far western Upper Peninsula, lies 630 highway miles (1,015 km) from Lambertville in the Lower Peninsula's southeastern corner. The geographic isolation of the Upper Peninsula from Michigan's political and population centers makes the U.P. culturally and economically distinct. Occasionally U.P. residents have called for secession from Michigan and establishment as a new state to be called "Superior."

Lower Peninsula

Little Traverse Bay at sunset, viewed from Petoskey

The Lower Peninsula, shaped like a mitten, is 277 miles (446 km) long from north to south and 195 miles (314 km) from east to west and occupies nearly two-thirds of the state's land area. The surface of the peninsula is generally level, broken by conical hills and glacial moraines usually not more than a few hundred feet tall. It is divided by a low water divide running north and south. The larger portion of the state is on the west of this and gradually slopes toward Lake Michigan. The highest point in the Lower Peninsula is either Briar Hill at 1,705 feet (520 m), or one of several points nearby in the vicinity of Cadillac. The lowest point is the surface of Lake Erie at 571 feet (174 m).

A feature of Michigan that gives it the distinct shape of a mitten is the Thumb. This peninsula projects out into Lake Huron and the Saginaw Bay. The geography of the Thumb is mainly flat with a few rolling hills. Other peninsulas of Michigan include the Keweenaw Peninsula, making up the Copper Country region of the state. The Leelanau Peninsula lies in the Northern Lower Michigan region. *See Also Michigan Regions*

Lakes

Little Sable Point Light south of Pentwater, Michigan.

Numerous lakes and marshes mark both peninsulas, and the coast is much indented. Keweenaw Bay, Whitefish Bay, and the Big and Little Bays De Noc are the principal indentations on the Upper Peninsula. The Grand and Little Traverse, Thunder, and Saginaw bays indent the Lower Peninsula. After Alaska, Michigan has the longest shoreline of any state—3,288 miles (5,326 km). An additional 1,056 miles (1,699 km) can be added if islands are included. This roughly equals the length of the Atlantic Coast from Maine to Florida.

The state has numerous large islands, the principal ones being the Manitou, Beaver, and Fox groups in Lake Michigan; Isle Royale and Grande Isle in Lake Superior; Drummond, Marquette, Bois Blanc, and Mackinac islands in Lake Huron; and Neebish and Sugar islands in St. Mary's River. Michigan has about 150 lighthouses, the most of any U.S. state. The first lighthouses in Michigan were built between 1818 and 1822. They were built to project light at night and to serve as a landmark during the day to safely guide the passenger ships and freighters traveling the Great Lakes. See Lighthouses in the United States.

The state's rivers are small, short and shallow, and few are navigable. The principal ones include the Au Sable, Thunder Bay, Cheboygan, and Saginaw, all of which flow into Lake Huron; the Ontonagon, and Tahquamenon, which flow into Lake Superior; and the St. Joseph, Kalamazoo, Grand, Muskegon, Manistee, and Escanaba, which flow into Lake Michigan. The state has 11,037 inland lakes and 38,575 square miles (62,067 km²) of Great Lakes waters and rivers in addition to 1305 square miles (3380 km^2) of inland water. No point in Michigan is more than six miles (10 km) from an inland lake or more than 85 miles (137 km) from one of the Great Lakes.

Protected lands

See also: List of Michigan state parks

The state is home to one national park: Isle Royale National Park, located in Lake Superior, about 30 miles (48 km) southeast of Thunder Bay, Ontario. Other national protected areas in the state include: Keweenaw National Historical Park, Pictured Rocks National Lakeshore, Sleeping Bear Dunes National Lakeshore, Huron National Forest, Manistee National Forest, Hiawatha National Forest, Ottawa National Forest, Fumee Lake Natural Area and Father Marquette National Memorial. The largest section of the North Country National Scenic Trail also passes through Michigan.

With 78 state parks, 19 state recreation areas, and 6 state forests, Michigan has the largest state park and state forest system of any state. These parks and forests include Holland State Park, Mackinac Island State Park, Au Sable State Forest, and Mackinaw State Forest.

Climate

Michigan has a humid continental climate, although there are two distinct regions. The southern and central parts of the Lower Peninsula (south of Saginaw Bay and from the Grand Rapids area southward) have a warmer climate (Koppen climate classification *Dfa*) with hot summers and cold winters. The northern part of Lower Peninsula and the entire Upper Peninsula has a more severe climate (Koppen *Dfb*), with warm, but shorter summers and longer, cold to very cold winters. Some parts of the state average high temperatures below freezing from December through February, and into early March in the far northern parts. During the winter through the middle of February the state is frequently subjected to heavy lake-effect snow. The state averages from 30-40 inches (75–100 cm) of precipitation annually.

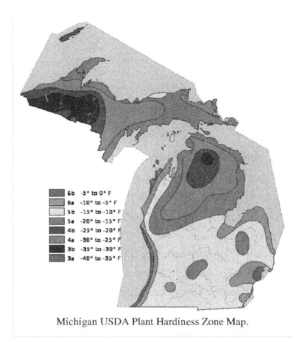

6b	-5° to 0° F
6a	-10° to -5° F
5b	-15° to -10° F
5a	-20° to -15° F
4b	-25° to -20° F
4a	-30° to -25° F
3b	-35° to -30° F
3a	-40° to -35° F

Michigan USDA Plant Hardiness Zone Map.

The entire state averages 30 days of thunderstorm activity per year. These can be severe, especially in the southern part of the state. The state averages 17 tornadoes per year, which are more common in the extreme southern portion of the state. Portions of the southern border have been nearly as vulnerable historically as parts of Tornado Alley. Farther north, in the Upper Peninsula, tornadoes are rare.

Monthly Normal High and Low Temperatures For Various Michigan Cities in °F(°C)												
City	Jan	Feb	Mar	Apr	May	Jun	Jul	Aug	Sep	Oct	Nov	Dec
Detroit	31/18	34/20	45/28	58/38	70/49	79/59	83/64	81/62	74/54	61/42	48/34	36/23
	(-1/-8)	(1/-7)	(7/-2)	(14/3)	(21/9)	(26/15)	(28/18)	(27/17)	(23/12)	(16/6)	(9/1)	(2/-5)
Flint	29/13	32/15	43/24	56/35	69/45	78/55	82/59	80/57	72/49	60/39	46/30	34/19
	(-2/-11)	(0/-9)	(6/-4)	(13/2)	(21/7)	(26/13)	(28/15)	(27/14)	(22/9)	(16/4)	(8/-1)	(1/-7)
Grand Rapids	29/16	33/17	43/26	57/36	70/47	78/56	82/60	80/59	72/51	60/40	46/31	34/21
	(-2/-9)	(1/-8)	(6/-3)	(14/2)	(21/8)	(26/13)	(28/16)	(27/15)	(22/11)	(11/4)	(8/-1)	(1/-6)
Lansing	29/14	33/15	44/24	57/34	69/45	78/54	82/58	80/57	72/49	60/39	46/30	34/20
	(-2/-10)	(1/-9)	(7/-4)	(14/1)	(21/7)	(26/12)	(28/14)	(27/14)	(22/9)	(16/4)	(8/-1)	(1/-7)
Marquette	20/3	24/5	33/14	46/27	62/39	70/48	75/54	73/52	63/44	51/34	35/22	24/10
	(-7/-16)	(-4/-15)	(1/-10)	(8/-3)	(17/4)	(21/9)	(24/12)	(23/11)	(17/7)	(11/1)	(2/-6)	(-4/-12)

Muskegon	30/17 (-1/-8)	32/18 (0/-8)	42/25 (6/-4)	55/35 (13/2)	67/45 (19/7)	76/54 (24/12)	80/60 (27/16)	78/59 (26/15)	70/51 (21/11)	59/41 (15/5)	46/32 (8/0)	35/23 (2/-5)
Sault Ste Marie	22/5 (-6/-15)	24/7 (-4/-14)	34/16 (1/-9)	48/29 (9/-2)	63/39 (17/4)	71/46 (22/7)	76/52 (24/11)	74/52 (23/11)	65/45 (18/7)	53/36 (12/2)	39/26 (12/-3)	27/13 (-3/-11)
[4]												

Geology

The geological formation of the state is greatly varied. Primary boulders are found over the entire surface of the Upper Peninsula (being principally of primitive origin), while Secondary deposits cover the entire Lower Peninsula. The Upper Peninsula exhibits Lower Silurian sandstones, limestones, copper and iron bearing rocks, corresponding to the Huronian system of Canada. The central portion of the Lower Peninsula contains coal measures and rocks of the Permo-Carboniferous period. Devonian and sub-Carboniferous deposits are scattered over the entire state.

The soil is of a varied composition and in large areas is very fertile, especially in the south. However, the Upper Peninsula

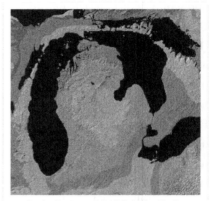

Geologic map of the Michigan Basin.

for the most part is rocky and mountainous, and the soil is unsuitable for agriculture. The climate is tempered by the proximity of the lakes and is much milder than in other locales with the same latitude. The principal forest trees include basswood, maple, elm, sassafras, butternut, walnut, poplar, hickory, oak, willow, pine, birch, beech, hemlock, witchhazel, tamarack, cedar, locust, dogwood, and ash.

List of Michigan state parks

This is a list of **Michigan state parks and related protected areas** under Michigan Department of Natural Resources and Environment (DNRE) jurisdiction. DNRE also operates 16 state harbors on the Great Lakes. Michigan's state parks system was started in 1919 and now contains 98 parks and recreation areas covering 285,000 acres (1,150 km²). There are 13,500 campsites in 142 campgrounds and 879 miles (1400 km) of trails. The parks received 21.2 million visitors in 2008.

Lake of the Clouds in Porcupine Mountains Wilderness State Park

Two Michigan state parks pre-date the creation of the park system in 1919. Michigan's first state park, Mackinac Island State Park, was created in 1895. It had served as the nation's second national park from 1875. In 1909 Michilimackinac State Park was created in nearby Mackinaw City. Both these parks, along with Historic Mill Creek State Park are under the jurisdiction of the Mackinac Island State Park Commission.

DNRE operates 746 boat launches on 57000 acres (230 km^2) of designated public water access sites. It also operates 16 "harbors of refuge" as well as providing support for the other 61 harbors in the system. The harbors of refuge are approximately 30 miles (50 km) apart along the Great Lakes shoreline to provide shelter from storms and often provide boat launches and supplies. There are 11 state underwater preserves covering 2450 square miles (6300 km^2) of Great Lakes bottomland and ten of them have a maritime museum or interpretive center in a nearby coastal community.

The state forest system consists of 4000000 acres (20000 km^2) of primarily working forest but also includes 138 campgrounds (including a dozen equestrian campgrounds). The Michigan state game and wildlife areas encompass more than 340000 acres (1400 km^2). DNRE also oversee the trail systems in the state. This includes 880 miles (1400 km) of non-motorized trails, 1145 miles (1800 km) of rail-trails, 3193 miles (5100 km) of off-road vehicle (ORV) routes and 6216 miles (10000 km) of snowmobile trails.

For a discussion of all protected areas in Michigan under all jurisdictions, see Protected areas of Michigan.

State parks

- Algonac State Park
- Aloha State Park
- Baraga State Park
- Bewabic State Park
- Brimley State Park
- Burt Lake State Park
- Cambridge Junction Historic State Park
- Cheboygan State Park
- Clear Lake State Park
- Coldwater Lake State Park
- Craig Lake State Park
- Dodge #4 State Park
- Duck Lake State Park
- Fayette Historic State Park
- Fisherman's Island State Park
- Fort Wilkins Historic State Park

Grand Mere State Park

- Grand Haven State Park
- Grand Mere State Park
- Harrisville State Park
- Hart-Montague Trail State Park
- Hartwick Pines State Park
- Hayes State Park
- Historic Mill Creek State Park
- Hoeft State Park (P.H. Hoeft)
- Hoffmaster State Park (P.J. Hoffmaster)
- Holland State Park
- Indian Lake State Park
- Interlochen State Park
- Kal-Haven Trail State Park
- Lake Gogebic State Park
- Lakelands Trail State Park
- Lakeport State Park
- Leelanau State Park

Holland State Park

- Ludington State Park
- Mackinac Island State Park and Fort Mackinac
- Maybury State Park
- McLain State Park (F.J. McLain)
- Mears State Park
- Meridian-Baseline State Park
- Colonial Michilimackinac and Old Mackinac Point Lighthouse
- Mitchell State Park
- Muskallonge Lake State Park
- Muskegon State Park
- Negwegon State Park
- Newaygo State Park
- North Higgins Lake State Park
- Onaway State Park
- Orchard Beach State Park
- Otsego Lake State Park
- Palms Book State Park
- Petoskey State Park
- Porcupine Mountains State Park
- Port Crescent State Park
- Sanilac Petroglyphs Historic State Park
- Saugatuck Dunes State Park
- Seven Lakes State Park

- Silver Lake State Park
- Sleeper State Park
- Sleepy Hollow State Park
- South Higgins Lake State Park
- Sterling State Park
- Straits State Park
- Tahquamenon Falls State Park
- Tawas Point State Park
- Thompson's Harbor State Park

Silver Lakes State Park

- Traverse City State Park
- Tri-Centennial State Park and Harbor
- Twin Lakes State Park
- Van Buren State Park

- Van Buren Trail State Park
- Van Riper State Park
- Warren Dunes State Park
- Warren Woods State Park
- Wells State Park
- White Pine Trail State Park
- Wilderness State Park
- Wilson State Park
- Young State Park

Recreation areas

- Bald Mountain Recreation Area
- Bass River Recreation Area
- Bay City Recreation Area
- Brighton Recreation Area
- Fort Custer Recreation Area
- Highland Recreation Area
- Holly Recreation Area
- Ionia State Recreation Area
- Island Lake Recreation Area
- Lake Hudson Recreation Area
- Metamora-Hadley Recreation Area
- Ortonville Recreation Area
- Pinckney Recreation Area
- Pontiac Lake Recreation Area
- Proud Lake State Recreation Area
- Rifle River Recreation Area

Proud Lake Recreation Area

- Waterloo Recreation Area
- Wetzel State Recreation Area
- Yankee Springs Recreation Area

State forests

- Au Sable State Forest
- Copper Country State Forest
- Escanaba River State Forest
- Lake Superior State Forest
- Mackinaw State Forest
- Pere Marquette State Forest

The Au Sable River runs through the Au Sable State Forest

Other sites

- Agate Falls Scenic Site
- Bond Falls Scenic Site
- Father Marquette National Memorial - a National Memorial under state supervision
- Laughing Whitefish Falls Scenic Site
- Ralph A. MacMullan Conference Center
- Sturgeon Point Scenic Site
- Wagner Falls Scenic Site

Wagner Falls

External links

- Michigan Department of Natural Resources [1]
- Map of Michigan State Parks [2]

List of National Historic Landmarks in Michigan

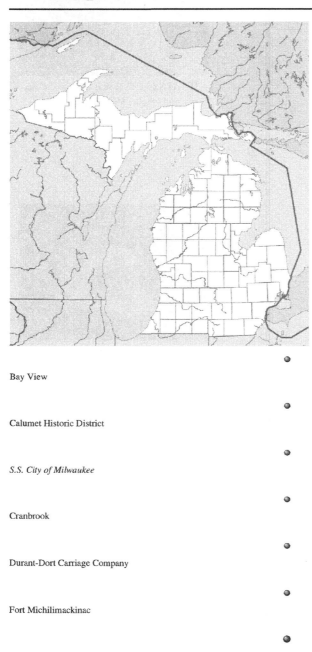

Bay View

Calumet Historic District

S.S. City of Milwaukee

Cranbrook

Durant-Dort Carriage Company

Fort Michilimackinac

Grand Hotel

Mackinac Island

Hemingway Cottage

Highland Ford Plant

Lightship No.103

St. Clair Tunnel

Marshall Historic District

State Capitol

Milwaukee Clipper

USS Silversides

Manitou Lifesaving Station

Norton Mounds

Quincy Mining Company

St. Ignace Mission

St. Mary's Falls Canal

Alden Dow House

Herbert H. Dow House

DETROIT

DETROIT NHLs:

Fisher Building

Columbia (Excursion Steamer)

Ford Piquette Ave. Plant

Fox Theater

General Motors Building

Guardian Building

Parke- Davis Laboratory

Pewabic Pottery

Edison Institute

Fair Lane

Ford River Rouge Complex

Michigan National Historic Landmarks (clickable map)

This is a complete **List of National Historic Landmarks in Michigan**, of which there are 34. The United States National Historic Landmark program is operated under the auspices of the National Park Service, and recognizes structures, districts, objects, and similar resources according to a list of criteria of national significance. The state of Michigan is home to 34 of these landmarks.

The table below lists all 34 of these sites, along with added detail and description.

In addition, two sites in Michigan were designated National Historic Landmarks, and subsequently de-designated. One other landmark, a movable object, has been relocated to another state. These three sites appear in another table further below.

Current NHLs in Michigan

	Landmark name	Image	Date of designation	Location	County	Description
1	Bay View		1987	Petoskey 45°23′08″N 84°55′49″W	Emmet	Established in 1876 as a Methodist camp meeting, this romantically-planned campground was converted to an independent chautauqua in 1885, a role it served until 1915. These two uniquely American community forms are exemplified in this extensive and well-preserved complex.
2	Calumet Historic District		1989	Calumet 47°14′45″N 88°27′14″W	Houghton	
3	*CITY OF MILWAUKEE* (Great Lakes Car Ferry)		1990	Manistee 44°15′34″N 86°18′58″W	Manistee	
4	*COLUMBIA* (Steamer)		1992	Detroit 42°19′29″N 83°02′38″W	Wayne	
5	Cranbrook		1989	Bloomfield Hills 42°34′23″N 83°14′57″W	Oakland	
6	Alden Dow House and Studio		1989	Midland 43°37′22″N 84°15′18″W	Midland	This house and studio were the residence and acknowledged masterpiece of 20th century architect Alden B. Dow. The quality and originality of his work, as well as his association with Frank Lloyd Wright, have earned him lasting national recognition.
7	Herbert H. Dow House		1976	Midland 43°37′08″N 84°15′10″W	Midland	A home of Herbert H. Dow
8	Durant-Dort Carriage Company Office		1978	Flint 43°01′03″N 83°41′43″W	Genesee	
9	Edison Institute (Greenfield Village and Henry Ford Museum)		1981	Dearborn 42°18′17″N 83°13′55″W	Wayne	

10	Fair Lane		1966k	Dearborn 42°18′51″N 83°13′57″W	Wayne	
11	Fisher Building		1989	Detroit 42°22′15″N 83°04′38″W	Wayne	Built in 1927 by the Fisher brothers, this skyscraper is one of the greatest works by architect Albert Kahn. The Fishers spent lavishly to make this Art Deco masterpiece a monumental gift to Detroit and one of the most finely detailed major commercial buildings in the United States.
12	Ford Piquette Avenue Plant		2006	Detroit 42°22′7″N 83°3′55″W	Wayne	
13	Ford River Rouge Complex		1978	Dearborn 42°18′34″N 83°09′44″W	Wayne	
14	Fort Michilimackinac		1960	Mackinaw City 45°47′11″N 84°44′8″W	Emmet	
15	Fox Theater (Detroit)		1989	Detroit 42°20′16″N 83°03′05″W	Wayne	
16	General Motors Building		1978	Detroit 42°22′09″N 83°04′32″W	Wayne	
17	Grand Hotel		1989	Mackinac Island 45°50′56″N 84°37′33″W	Mackinac	
18	Guardian Building		1989	Detroit 42°19′45″N 83°02′46″W	Wayne	
19	Ernest Hemingway Cottage		1968	Walloon Lake 45°16′41″N 84°59′58″W	Emmet	Boyhood summer home of author Ernest Hemingway. His father built the house in 1900 when his son was a year old, and it was here the future writer learned to hunt and fish and appreciate the outdoor life he came to celebrate in his writings.

20	Highland Park Ford Plant		1978	Highland Park 42°24′38″N 83°06′02″W	Wayne	
21	LIGHTSHIP NO. 103 "*HURON*"		December 20, 1989	Port Huron 42°59′15″N 82°25′36″W	St. Clair	
22	Mackinac Island		1960	Mackinac Island 45°52′N 84°38′W	Mackinac	This island's key role in the early fur trade was secured by its location at the center of the Great Lakes region. Hosting the northern headquarters of John Jacob Astor's American Fur Company until the 1840s, it preserves numerous buildings relating to the fur industry. Its geopolitical importance is illustrated at Fort Mackinac; control of this strategic island was not settled until the 1814 Treaty of Ghent.
23	Marshall Historic District		1991	Marshall 42°16′19″N 84°57′51″W	Calhoun	
24	Michigan State Capitol		1992	Lansing 42°44′01″N 84°33′14″W	Ingham	
25	*MILWAUKEE CLIPPER* (Passenger Steamship)		1989	Muskegon	Muskegon	
26	North Manitou Island Lifesaving Station		1998	Sleeping Bear Dunes National Lakeshore 45°07′09″N 85°58′39″W	Leelanau	
27	Norton Mound Group		1965	Grand Rapids	Kent	Center of Hopewellian culture in the western Great Lakes region, from ca. 400 B.C. to A.D. 400.

28	Parke-Davis Research Laboratory		1976	Detroit 42°20′06″N 83°00′52″W	Wayne	Built in 1902, this was the first industrial research laboratory in the U.S. established for the specific purpose of conducting pharmacological research, inaugurating the commercial pure science approach which has driven the rapid development of pharmaceutical technology. National Park Service staff recommended withdrawal of landmark status in 2002 due to loss of the building's historic integrity during conversion to a hotel.
29	Pewabic Pottery		1991	Detroit 42°21′42″N 82°58′52″W	Wayne	This 1907 building, designed by William Stratton, is the home of ceramic artist Mary Chase Perry Stratton's studio and production facilities. Her work in the Arts and Crafts movement raised the artistic standard of American pottery, and is featured architecturally or curatorially in numerous prominent buildings and distinguished institutions.
30	Quincy Mining Company Historic District		1989	Hancock 47°8′7″N 88°34′33″W	Houghton	
31	St. Clair River Tunnel		1993	Port Huron 42°57′29″N 82°25′59″W	St. Clair	
32	St. Ignace Mission		1960	St. Ignace 45°52′11″N 84°44′38″W	Mackinac	Now a park, this was the site of a mission established by Père Jacques Marquette, and the site of his grave in 1677. A second mission was established at a different site in 1837, and moved here in 1954.
33	St. Mary's Falls Canal		1966	Sault Ste. Marie 46°30′11″N 84°21′17″W	Chippewa	
34	USS SILVERSIDES (Submarine)		1986	Muskegon	Muskegon	

Former NHLs in Michigan

Landmark name	Image	Year listed	Locality	County	Description
Lincoln Motor Company Plant		1978, withdrawn 2005	Detroit	Wayne	Henry M. Leland acquired a factory here in 1917 and greatly expanded it in order to produce Liberty Engines as part of the World War I war effort. After the war, Leland used his long and prominent experience with Cadillac to inaugurate the Lincoln line of automobiles. Leland sold his company to Henry Ford in 1922; by 1952 this original Lincoln plant was retired from automotive production. Most of the complex was demolished in 2002/03, leading to withdrawal of its landmark designation.
Reo Motor Car Company Plant		1978, withdrawn 1985	Lansing	Ingham	In his third venture in the automotive industry, and after his departure from the highly successful Oldsmobile, Ransom E. Olds established the Reo Motor Car Company at this plant in 1904. Reo enjoyed early success and was responsible for many innovations in automobile manufacturing, but remained a niche company for most of its existence. The factory complex was demolished in 1980 to make way for site redevelopment, and landmark status was withdrawn in 1985.
Ste. Claire (passenger steamboat)		1992	Ecorse (formerly)	Wayne (formerly)	Relocated to Ohio.

See also

- List of Registered Historic Places in Michigan
- List of U.S. National Historic Landmarks by state
- Detroit Historical Museum
- Historic preservation
- History of Michigan
- Michigan Department of History, Arts and Libraries
- Michigan History magazine
- National Register of Historic Places

External links

- National Historic Landmark Program [1] at the National Park Service
- Lists of National Historic Landmarks [2]

Overview of Troy

Troy, Michigan

Troy, Michigan	
— City —	
Motto: *The City of Tomorrow, Today*	
Location in the state of Michigan	
Coordinates: 42°34′49″N 83°8′35″W	
Country	United States
State	Michigan
County	Oakland
Government	
- Type	Council-Manager
- Mayor	Louise Schilling
- City manager	John Szerlag
Area	
- City	33.6 sq mi (87.1 km^2)
- Land	33.5 sq mi (86.9 km^2)
- Water	0.1 sq mi (0.3 km^2)
Elevation	748 ft (228 m)

Population (2000)	
- City	80959
- Density	2413.9/sq mi (932.0/km^2)
- Metro	5456428
Time zone	EST (UTC-5)
- Summer (DST)	EDT (UTC-4)
ZIP codes	48007, 48083, 48084, 48085, 48098, 48099
Area code(s)	248
FIPS code	26-80700
GNIS feature ID	1615125
Website	http://www.troymi.gov

Troy is an affluent city in Oakland County in the U.S. state of Michigan. It is a suburb of Detroit. The population was 80,959 at the 2000 census, making it the 12th-largest city in Michigan by population, and the second-largest city in Oakland County after Farmington Hills. Troy has become a business and shopping destination in the Metro Detroit area, with numerous office centers and the upscale Somerset Collection mall.

Troy was recently ranked the 5th safest city in the nation, as well as the safest in Michigan. In 2008, Troy was ranked 22nd on a list of "Best Places to Live" in the United States by CNN Money, using criteria including housing, quality of education, economic strength, and recreational opportunities. In 2008, Troy ranked as the fourth most affordable U.S. city with a median household income of $90,000.

History

The first land purchases in what became Troy Township were recorded in 1819 in section 19. The first settlement, known as Troy Corners, originated two years later when Johnson Niles purchased 160 acres (65 ha) in what is now the north-central portion of the city. Four years later, Ira Smith built the first house at Big Beaver Corners, and the first public school opened at Troy Corners. Troy Township was organized on May 28, 1827. The City of Troy was incorporated in 1955, mainly as a way to prevent neighboring cities (Clawson, Royal Oak, and Birmingham) from incorporating any more of its land into their cities.

In 1966, I-75 was completed in Troy, which increased access to and from the city. This gave a major boost to Troy's economy, leading to the development of its civic center, school district, and recreation system.

Geography

According to the United States Census Bureau, the city has a total area of 33.6 square miles (87.1 km²)—33.5 square miles (86.9 km²) of it is land and 0.1 square miles (0.3 km²) of it (0.30%) is water. The latitude of Troy is 42.605N, and the longitude is -83.15W. It is in the Eastern Standard time zone. The mean elevation is 748 feet.

Culture

The Troy Historical Museum is a town-square-like museum chronicling the different stages of Troy's progression from first inhabitation to the city it has become today. Located at the corners of Livernois Road and Wattles Road, the museum is located behind the old city hall building. Open year round, the museum has ten original, complete structures which patrons may enter and observe how they functioned in the past and how they were decorated, as all buildings are full of artifacts from that period. Each structure is original and was painstakingly moved from its original location to the museum intact. Starting with a log and mud structure used by the first settlers, there is also an 18th century schoolhouse and estate, a general store, a blacksmith's shop, a church along with the pastor's home, and the old city hall, which acts as a general museum. There is a gazebo in the center of the square which will host parties and period bands during annual festivities. Many schools from around the area plan field trips to the museum, and the church is also available for weddings.

In the summer of 2005, to commemorate the city's 50th anniversary, ceramic beaver statues, each standing four feet (1.2 m) high, were displayed at various locations in the city. The beaver is the symbol of Troy, and the city's main commercial thoroughfare (Big Beaver Road) is named for it.

Sports

In 2003, Troy was named Michigan's Sportstown by *Sports Illustrated* magazine for having the top community sports programs in the state. Troy is home to the Troy Sports Center, which is the official training facility of the Detroit Red Wings of the NHL. The facility is also used for indoor soccer and hockey leagues, and is home to the city's high school hockey teams.

Media

In addition to the Detroit News and Detroit Free Press, regional newspapers serving all of southeast Michigan, the city is served by the Daily Tribune(published daily), the Observer & Eccentric (which is published twice a week), the Troy Beacon [1](published every Thursday), the Troy Times, and the Troy-Somerset Gazette [2].

Economy

See also: Pavilions of Troy and Economy of metropolitan Detroit

Troy is a thriving center of business, particularly in the automotive and financial sectors, and is home to a number of major companies. Based on property value, Troy is the second largest city in Michigan, second only to Detroit. Troy is home to the upscale Somerset Collection mall, featuring a skywalk and over 180 stores, and the Oakland Mall. The Top of Troy is the city's tallest building with offices of PNC Financial Services. Bank of America maintains a major operations center in Troy.

Planners have proposed the Pavilions of Troy project for the city, a landscaped square with boulevards lined with upscale shops, restaurants, offices, a theater, and condominiums.

Major companies

Further information: List of Michigan companies

- Altair Engineering
- ArvinMeritor
- Bank of America (major center)
- Budd Company
- Delphi Corporation
- DuPont Automotive
- Entertainment Publications
- Flagstar Bancorp, Inc.
- J.D. Power and Associates
- Kelly Services
- The Kresge Foundation
- Magna Powertrain
- Olga's Kitchen
- Rexair LLC
- Saleen Special Vehicles
- SAE International

The Top of Troy.

- Specter Werkes/Sports
- Starz Home Entertainment
- Syntel
- The Woodbridge Company (US Headquarters)
- Ziebart

^ Arbor Drugs was headquartered in Troy until it was acquired by CVS Corporation in 1998 for an estimated $1.48 billion, in the process making CVS the nation's largest chain-drug retailer.

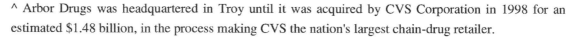

^^ Frank's Nursery & Crafts was an arts and crafts chain spanning 14 states that was headquartered in Troy, even after being acquired by General Host Corporation in 1983. The company filed for bankruptcy in 2004, and became defunct soon after.

^^^Kmart was headquartered in Troy until it acquired Sears in 2005, establishing itself in the former Sears headquarters in Hoffman Estates, Illinois. Its massive headquarters still remains, though it is scheduled for demolition and the creation of a landscaped square with boulevards lined with upscale shops, restaurants, offices, a theater, and condominiums..

Demographics

As of the census of 2000, there were 80,959 people, 30,018 households, and 21,883 families residing in the city. The population density was 2,413.9 people per square mile (932.0/km²). There were 30,872 housing units at an average density of 920.5 per square mile (355.4/km²). The racial makeup of the city was 82.30% White, 2.09% African American, 0.15% Native American, 13.25% Asian, 0.02% Pacific Islander, 0.36% from other races, and 1.82% from two or more races. 1.46% of the population is Hispanic or Latino of any race. Troy has the highest percentage of people of Asian descent of any city in Michigan.

There were 30,018 households out of which 36.9% had children under the age of 18 living with them, 64.5% were married couples living together, 6.0% had a female householder with no husband present, and 27.1% were non-families. 22.8% of all households were made up of individuals and 7.8% had someone living alone who was 65 years of age or older. The average household size was 2.69 and the average family size was 3.23.

In the city the population was spread out with 26.2% under the age of 18, 6.7% from 18 to 24, 29.8% from 25 to 44, 27.1% from 45 to 64, and 10.2% who were 65 years of age or older. The median age was 38 years. For every 100 females there were 98.1 males. For every 100 females age 18 and over, there were 94.8 males.

According to a 2007 estimate, the median income for a household in the city was $84,330, and the median income for a family was $101,271. Males had a median income of $66,475 versus $41,026 for females. The per capita income for the city was $35,936. About 1.7% of families and 2.7% of the population were below the poverty line, including 2.2% of those under age 18 and 5.5% of those age 65 or over.

Government

Troy uses the Council-Manager form of government, and thus is governed by a City Council consisting of a Mayor and six council members. The city council appoints a City Manager, who manages the day-to-day operations of the city.

The City of Troy and City of Clawson on its southern border compose Michigan's 41st District for State Representative. The district has been represented in the State House by Marty Knollenberg since 2007, and in the state Senate by John Pappageorge, also since 2007. On the national level, Troy is part of the 9th district, represented by Joe Knollenberg from 1993–2009 and now Gary Peters, who defeated Knollenberg in a highly-publicized race in November 2008.

Education

Troy is home to International Academy of Design and Technology, Walsh College, a business oriented school, as well as branches for the University of Phoenix, Central Michigan University, Spring Arbor University, and ITT Technical Institute. Michigan State University also has its Management Education Center located off of I-75 near the intersection of Crooks Rd. and Square Lake Rd. (19 Mile).

Troy is well known for its exemplary schools both in Michigan and nationally. The Troy School District has six national blue ribbon and 13 State Exemplary Schools. The schools have a 99% graduation rate, with 95% of those students going on to higher education and 2% going on to military service. Both Troy High School and Athens High School were named to the list of The 1000 Most Outstanding High Schools in the United States by Newsweek magazine.

The Troy School District also sends 75 students per year to the International Academy, currently ranked 7th in the Newsweek rankings of the best public high schools in the United States. Troy has hosted the International Academy's eastern campus in the old Baker Middle School beginning with the 2008-2009 school year.

The public schools comprising the Troy School District are as follows:

Elementary

- Costello
- Hamilton
- Hill
- Bemis
- Leonard
- Martell
- Morse
- Barnard
- Schroeder
- Troy Union

- Wass
- Wattles

Middle

- Baker
- Boulan
- Larson
- Smith

High

- Athens
- Troy
- Niles Community High School
- International Academy East

The private schools are:

- Bethany Christian School

Transportation

Further information: Transportation in metropolitan Detroit

Oakland-Troy Airport

Oakland-Troy Airport (IATA: VLL, ICAO: KVLL), formerly (IATA: 7D2, ICAO: K7D2) is a small suburban general aviation airport operated by Oakland County and has a single 3,550 feet x 60 feet (1082 m x 18 m) paved runway.

The Oakland-Troy Airport is considered the County's 'executive' airport. Business travelers and tourists using private, corporate and charter aircraft benefit from the airport's convenient proximity to business, recreation and entertainment facilities. It is located between Maple Road and 14 Mile Road.

Charter passenger, air freight, as well as aircraft maintenance and fuel, are available on the field.

Troy was also home to the Big Beaver Airport, (IATA: 3BB), which was located at the corners of Big Beaver Road and John R Road. It opened in 1946 and closed in 1995 due to declining use and pressure to sell the land for commercial development.

Roads and freeways

Further information: Roads and freeways in metropolitan Detroit

- **75** I-75 cuts through the middle of Troy from the north-west corner bordering Bloomfield Township, and continuing southward towards the south-east border of the city entering Madison Heights. Exit numbers 65, 67, 69, and 72 directly service Troy.

Mile Roads

Main article: Mile Road System (Detroit)

- 14 Mile Road (Southern-most border with Madison Heights)
- 15 Mile Road - Maple Road
- 16 Mile Road - Big Beaver Road
- 17 Mile Road - Wattles Road
- 18 Mile Road - Long Lake Road
- 19 Mile Road - Square Lake Road
- 20 Mile Road - South Boulevard (Northern-most border with Rochester Hills)

Notable people

Further information: People from Detroit

- Sean Collins, NHL defensemen for the Hershey Bears and signed to the Washington Capitals
- Joe Faris, Contestant on Project Runway (season 5)
- Hunter Foster, Tony Award-nominated actor/singer; librettist and playwright
- Sutton Foster, Tony Award-winning Broadway actress/singer/dancer
- Ellen Hollman, film and television actress
- Robert J. Huber, mayor of Troy from 1959–1964, state senator and congressman
- Martin Klebba, actor, known from *Pirates of the Caribbean* films and Scrubs (TV series)
- Steve McCatty, former MLB pitcher and coach
- Ivana Miličević, television and film actress
- Tomo Miličević, guitarist, *30 Seconds to Mars*
- Bridget Regan, musician, Flogging Molly
- Hugh W. Sloan, Jr., Watergate figure
- Stillwater, fictional rock band from the film *Almost Famous*
- Aileen Wuornos, serial killer, executed, basis for the 2003 film *Monster*

See also

- Birmingham, Michigan
- Bloomfield Hills, Michigan

External links

- Official website [3]
- Troy School District [4]
- Troy Public Library [5]

Oakland County, Michigan

Oakland County, Michigan
Seal
Location in the state of Michigan
Michigan's location in the U.S.

Founded	January 12, 1819
Seat	Pontiac
Area - Total - Land - Water	908 sq mi (2352 km²) 873 sq mi (2260 km²) 35 sq mi (92 km²), 3.91%
Population - (2000) - Density	1194156 1391/sq mi (537/km²)
Website	www.OakGov.Com [1]

Oakland County is a county in the U.S. state of Michigan. As of 2009, the population was estimated at 1,205,508. The county seat is Pontiac. Oakland County is part of the Detroit metropolitan area; though the city of Detroit is located in neighboring Wayne County, south of 8 Mile Road. Oakland County is home to 62 cities, villages and townships. These communities range from blue-collar, inner-ring suburbs like Ferndale and Hazel Park, to wealthy cities such as Farmington Hills, Troy, Birmingham,

Bloomfield Hills, Walled Lake, Novi, West Bloomfield Township, Rochester Hills, and Oakland Charter Township. The white-collar cities of Troy, Southfield, Farmington Hills, and Auburn Hills host a diverse mix of Fortune 500 companies. The cities of Royal Oak, home of the Detroit Zoological Park, and Ferndale attract many young people to their mature, bohemian downtowns, which have many restaurants, shops and night clubs. Oakland County is also home to Oakland University, a large public institution that straddles the Auburn Hills and Rochester Hills border.

Metro Detroit's suburbs are among the most affluent in the nation. Oakland County is the 4th wealthiest county in the United States among counties with more than one million people. The county's knowledge-based economic initiative, coined "Automation Alley", is one of the largest employment centers for engineering and related occupations in the United States. Oakland County has shared in the recent economic hardships brought on by troubles at General Motors, Ford, and Chrysler, although it has fared better than Detroit and Flint, as its economy is more diverse and less reliant on manufacturing jobs. All three automotive companies are major employers within southeast Michigan and have a significant presence within Oakland County.

Geography

According to the U.S. Census Bureau, the county has a total area of 908 square miles (2,352 km²). Of that, 873 square miles (2,260 km²) of it is land and 35 square miles (92 km²) of it (3.91%) is water.

Oakland County was originally divided into 25 separate townships, which are listed below. Each township is roughly equal in size at six miles (10 km) by six miles, for a total township area of 36 square miles (93 km^2). The roots of this design were born out of the Land Ordinance of 1785 and the subsequent Northwest Ordinance of 1787. Oakland County itself is a prime example of the land policy that was established, as all townships are equal in size (save for slight variations due to waterways). Section 16 in each township was reserved for financing and maintaining public education, and even today many schools in Oakland County townships are located within that section.

Wayne County, where the city of Detroit is located, borders Oakland County to the south. The southern boundary is 8 Mile Road, also known as "Baseline Road" in some areas. The baseline was used during the original surveying for Michigan, and it serves as the northern/southern boundaries for counties from Lake St. Clair all the way to Lake Michigan. This divide (8 Mile Road) has been widely known as an unofficial racial dividing line between the largely black city and almost exclusively white suburbs. Some exceptions to this pattern of *de facto* segregation have developed in recent years, as middle-class African-Americans depart the city for inner-ring suburbs, notably Southfield, west of Woodward Avenue, but to the east the line has endured.

Adjacent counties

- Lapeer County (northeast)
- Genesee County (northwest)
- Macomb County (east)
- Wayne County (southeast)
- Washtenaw County (southwest)
- Livingston County (west)

Demographics

Historical populations		
Census	Pop.	%±
1900	44792	—
1910	49576	10.7%
1920	90050	81.6%
1930	211251	134.6%
1940	254068	20.3%
1950	396001	55.9%
1960	690259	74.3%
1970	907871	31.5%
1980	1011793	11.4%
1990	1083592	7.1%
2000	1194156	10.2%
Est. 2008	1202174	0.7%

As of the census of 2000, there were 1,194,156 people, 471,115 households, and 315,175 families residing in the county. The population density was 1,369 people per square mile (528/km²). There were 492,006 housing units at an average density of 564 per square mile (218/km²). The racial makeup of the county was 82.75% White, 10.11% Black or African American, 0.27% Native American, 4.14% Asian American, 0.02% Pacific Islander, 0.84% from other races, and 1.86% from two or more races. 2.43% of the population were Hispanic or Latino of any race. Regarding ancestry, 14.4% were German, 9.0% Irish, 8.5% English, 8.5% Polish, 5.7% Italian and 5.5% American, according to Census 2000. 87.4% spoke English, 2.0% Spanish, 1.3% Syriac and 1.0% Arabic as their first language.

The 2000 census showed two Native American tribes with more than 1,000 members in Oakland County. There were 2,095 Cherokee and 1,458 Chippewa.

The Jewish community of metropolitan Detroit, with a population of 72,000, is the 21st largest Jewish community in the nation. This community is concentrated in Oakland County, especially in West Bloomfield, Bloomfield Hills, Farmington Hills and Huntington Woods.

There were 471,115 households, of which 32.40% had children under the age of 18 living with them. 54.20% were married couples living together, 9.50% had a female householder with no husband present, and 33.10% were non-families. 27.30% of all households were made up of individuals and 8.50% had someone living alone who was 65 years of age or older. The average household size was 2.51 and the average family size was 3.09.

Among Asian-Americans, eight ethnic groups had more than 1,000 members in the county. The most numerous were those of Asian Indian decent, with 20,705. Next were those of Chinese heritage, numbering 10,018. Next were those of Japanese (5,589), Filipino (5,450) Korean (5,351), Vietnamese (1,687), Pakistani (1,458) and Hmong (1,210) ancestry.

The county's population was spread out in terms of age, with 25.20% of people under the age of 18, 7.20% from 18 to 24, 32.40% from 25 to 44, 23.90% from 45 to 64, and 11.30% who were 65 years of age or older. The median age was 37 years. For every 100 females there were 95.90 males. For every 100 females age 18 and over, there were 92.70 males.

The median income for a household in the county was $61,907, and the median income for a family was $75,540 (these figures had risen to $67,619 and $85,468 respectively as of a 2007 estimate). Males had a median income of $55,833 versus $35,890 for females. The per capita income for the county was $32,534. About 3.80% of families and 5.50% of the population were below the poverty line, including 6.50% of those under age 18 and 6.50% of those age 65 or over.

In 2005, the U.S. Census Bureau estimated that non-Hispanic whites (including Arabs and Chaldeans) formed 78.6% of the population; African-Americans, 11.8%; Asian-Americans, 5.3%; and Hispanic or Latino people (of any race), 2.8%.

History

Created by territorial Gov. Lewis Cass in 1819, sparsely settled Oakland was twice its current size at first, but shrank as Michigan's population grew and new counties were established. Woodward Avenue and the Detroit and Pontiac Railroad helped draw settlers in the 1840s. By 1840, Oakland had more than fifty mills. Pontiac, located on the Clinton River, was Oakland's first town and became the county seat. After the Civil War, Oakland was mainly an agricultural county with numerous isolated villages. By the end of the 19th century, three rail lines served Pontiac and the city attracted carriage and wagon factories. Streetcars began moving people in the late 1890s.

Developers turned southern Oakland County into a suburb of Detroit in the 1890s, when a Cincinnati firm platted a section of Royal Oak called "Urbanrest." Migration worked both ways. Several thousand people moved from Oakland County farms to Detroit as the city attracted factories. By 1910, a number of rich Detroiters had summer homes and some year-round residences in what became Bloomfield Hills. The auto age enveloped Pontiac in the early 1900s. The Oakland Motor Car Co. was founded in 1907 and became a part of General Motors Corp., which was soon Pontiac's dominant firm.

In the 1950s, jobs and people began leaving Detroit. Northland Center opened in 1954. Oakland County passed Wayne County in effective buying power by 1961, when it ranked 28th in the nation in household income. It ranked second-highest nationally in per capita income for counties of more than a million people, behind New York County (Manhattan). The median price of a home in Oakland County skyrocketed to $164,697, more than $30,000 above the national median.

Government

The county government operates the jail, operates the major local courts, keeps files of deeds and mortgages, maintains vital records, administers public health regulations, and participates with the state in the provision of welfare and other social services. The county board of commissioners controls the budget but has limited authority to make laws or ordinances. In Michigan, most local government functions — police and fire, building and zoning, tax assessment, street maintenance, etc. — are the responsibility of individual cities and townships. Oakland County has an elected sheriff, and his or her law-enforcement services are used throughout the county. Fourteen cities/townships do not have personalized police forces, but rather contract with the sheriff for police services specific to the municipalities. For instance, the city of Rochester Hills does not have a "Rochester Hills Police Department," but instead has an established sheriff substation in the city with deputies who are dedicated to that city only. That branch operates as the Oakland County Sheriff's Department, Rochester Hills substation. The sheriff operates in the same manner with other municipalities who opt not to have their own police agencies. This typically is a cost-effective way for municipalities to provide police services to its citizens. The county sheriff also maintains a civil division, marine division, alcohol and traffic enforcement units, and an aviation division.

Roads that are not maintained by a local community (city/village) are maintained by the Road Commission for Oakland County [2], which is governed by three board members appointed by the Oakland County Board of Commissioners.

Oakland County elected officials

- County Executive: L. Brooks Patterson (Republican)
- Prosecuting Attorney: Jessica R. Cooper (Democrat)
- Sheriff: Mike Bouchard (Republican)
- County Clerk/Register of Deeds: Ruth Johnson (Republican)
- County Treasurer: Andy Meisner (Democrat)
- Water Resources Commissioner: John P. McCulloch (Republican)
- Board of Commissioners: 25 members, elected from districts (13 Republicans, 12 Democrats)

(information as of January 2010)

Politics

Presidential Election Results 1960-2008

Year	Democrat	Republican
2008	**56.42%** *373,270*	41.94% *277,480*
2004	**49.75%** *319,387*	49.32% *316,633*
2000	**49.31%** *281,201*	48.10% *274,319*
1996	**47.84%** *241,884*	43.48% *219,855*
1992	38.64% *214,733*	**43.57%** *242,160*
1988	37.78% *174,745*	**61.27%** *283,359*
1984	32.76% *150,286*	**66.71%** *306,050*
1980	35.58% *164,869*	**54.65%** *253,211*
1976	39.47% *164,266*	**58.69%** *244,271*
1972	34.16% *129,400*	**63.78%** *241,613*
1968	44.76% *154,630*	**45.31%** *156,538*
1964	**61.44%** *182,797*	38.33% *114,025*
1960	45.39% *135,531*	**54.27%** *162,026*

Oakland County historically has been a stronghold of the Republican Party, in large part because of the party's support for policies that favor businesses. However, the county also contains a sizable number of unaffiliated voters, many of whom have recently favored the Democratic Party. In the 1990s, Oakland County moved toward the Democratic Party at the national level. Political analyst Michael Barone, among others, has theorized that this occurred when cultural issues such as abortion rights and gun control became more salient than economic concerns for more voters, especially affluent suburban women. Democratic presidential candidates won a plurality of the county's vote in 1996, 2000 and 2004, and a majority in 2008 (*See chart at right*).

In the 111th Congress, Oakland County is represented by two Democrats, Gary Peters and Sander Levin, and two Republicans, Thaddeus McCotter and Mike Rogers. Peters was elected for the first time 2008, a victory that was seen as a particular coup for the Democrats as his seat, the 9th, had been held by Republicans for over twenty years.

Cities, villages, and townships

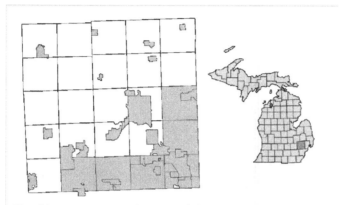

The white areas represent unincorporated charter and civil townships. The gray areas represent incorporated cities and villages.

Cities

- Auburn Hills
- Berkley
- Birmingham
- Bloomfield Hills
- Clarkston
- Clawson
- Farmington
- Farmington Hills [1]
- Ferndale
- Hazel Park
- Huntington Woods
- Keego Harbor
- Lake Angelus
- Lathrup Village
- Madison Heights
- Novi
- Oak Park
- Orchard Lake Village
- Pleasant Ridge
- Pontiac (county seat)
- Rochester
- Rochester Hills
- Royal Oak
- South Lyon
- Southfield
- Sylvan Lake
- Troy [1]
- Walled Lake
- Wixom

[1]In the 2000 Census, Farmington Hills was the most populous city in the county. As of the 2005 Census estimates, Troy is now the most populous city.

Villages

- Beverly Hills
- Bingham Farms
- Franklin
- Holly
- Lake Orion
- Leonard
- Milford
- Ortonville
- Oxford
- Wolverine Lake

Townships

• Addison Township	• Oakland Charter Township
• Avon Township*	• Orion Charter Township
• Bloomfield Charter Township	• Oxford Charter Township
• Brandon Township	• Pontiac Township*
• Commerce Charter Township	• Rose Township
• Farmington Township*	• Royal Oak Charter Township
• Groveland Township	• Southfield Township
• Highland Charter Township	• Springfield Township
• Holly Township	• Troy Township*
• Independence Charter Township	• Waterford Charter Township
• Lyon Charter Township	• West Bloomfield Charter Township
• Milford Charter Township	• White Lake Township
• Novi Township	

* Township has been incorporated into a city: Avon to the City of Rochester Hills, Farmington to the City of Farmington Hills, Pontiac to the City of Pontiac, City of Lake Angelus and City of Auburn Hills, and Troy to the City of Troy. For survey purposes, these areas are still referred to by the assigned township name.

Transportation

Air

- Coleman A. Young International Airport (DET) (Detroit) - General aviation only. This airport is in neighboring Wayne County in the city of Detroit.
- Detroit Metropolitan Wayne County Airport (DTW) (Romulus) - Major commercial airport, hub for Delta Air Lines and Spirit Airlines; located in Wayne County.
- Flint-Bishop International Airport(FNT) (Flint) - Commercial airport, which is located in neighboring Genesee County.
- Oakland County International Airport (PTK) Waterford Township) - Charter passenger facility.

Major highways

75	(Walter P. Chrysler Freeway) is the main north-south route in the region, serving Flint, Pontiac, Troy, and Detroit, before continuing south (as the Fisher and Detoit-Toledo Freeways) to serve many of the communities along the shore of Lake Erie.
96	runs northwest-southeast through Oakland County and (as the Jeffries Freeway) has its eastern terminus in downtown Detroit.
275	runs north-south from I-75 in the south to the junction of I-96 and I-696 in the north, providing a bypass through the western suburbs of Detroit.
696	(Walter P. Reuther Freeway) runs east-west from the junction of I-96 and I-275, providing a route through the northern suburbs of Detroit. Taken together, I-275 and I-696 form a semicircle around Detroit.
24	US-24 ends north of Pontiac at I-75. To the south, US 24 serves suburban Detroit and Monroe before entering Ohio. Much of US 24 in Oakland County is named Telegraph Road (US 24), and it is a major north-south road extending from Toledo, Ohio through Monroe, Wayne, and Oakland Counties to Pontiac. It gained notoriety in a song (*Telegraph Road*) by the group Dire Straits.
1	M-1 (Woodward Avenue) has a northern terminus in Pontiac. The route continues southerly from Oakland County into the City of Detroit, ending downtown. The Detroit Zoo is located along M-1 in Oakland County. M-1 is also home to the Woodward Dream Cruise, a classic-car cruise from Pontiac to Ferndale that is held in August. It is the largest single-day classic-car cruise in America.
5	M-5
10	M-10: The John C. Lodge Freeway runs largely parallel to I-75 from Southfield to downtown Detroit.
15	M-15 (Ortonville Road, Main St. in Clarkston)
24	M-24 (Lapeer Road) has a southern terminus at I-75 north of Pontiac. To the north, the route continues to Lapeer and beyond. Note: M-24 and US 24 do not intersect at present, although this was the case until the 1950s.
39	M-39: The Southfield Freeway runs north-south from Southfield to Allen Park from I-94. North of 10 Mile Road, the freeway ends and continues as Southfield Road into Birmingham.

	M-59 (Highland Road [from Pontiac westerly], Huron Street [within Pontiac] and Veterans Memorial Freeway [Pontiac to Utica]), continues east in Macomb County as Hall Road to Clinton Township and west to I-96 near Howell
	M-102 Perhaps better known as 8 Mile Road, M-102 follows the Oakland/Wayne County boundary line for most of its length. 8 Mile Road, known by many due to the film *8 Mile*, forms the dividing line between Detroit on the south and the suburbs of Macomb and Oakland counties on the north. It is also known as Baseline Road outside of Detroit, because it coincides with the baseline used in surveying Michigan; that baseline is also the boundary for a number of Michigan counties, as well as the boundary for Illinois and Wisconsin. It is designated as M-102 for much of its length in Wayne County.
	M-150 (Rochester Road) serves as a spur highway from M-59 into the city of Rochester.

Other major roads

- Grand River Avenue connects the suburbs of Brighton, Novi, and Farmington to downtown Detroit. The avenue follows the route of old U.S. Route 16, before I-96 replaced it in 1962. It is one of the five roads planned by Judge August Woodward to radiate out from Detroit and connect the city to other parts of the state.

Mile roads

- Surface-street navigation in metro Detroit is commonly anchored by "mile roads," major east-west surface streets that are spaced at one-mile (1.6 km) intervals and increment as one travels north and away from the city center. Mile roads sometimes have two names, the numeric name (e.g., 15 Mile Road), used in Macomb County, and a local name (e.g., Maple Road), used in Oakland County (for the most part). Main article: Mile Road System (Detroit)

Bicycling

The conditions on most non-residential roads in Oakland County are not favorable to bicycling. Exceptions to this are primarily in the inner-ring suburbs within the southeast corner of the county. This is due to their street grid.

A primary reason for these unfavorable cycling conditions is the Road Commission for Oakland County has a policy of not accommodating bicycles on the road. As a result, some communities have designated sidepaths (locally called "safety paths") as bike routes which do not meet the American Association of State Highway and Transportation Officials (AASHTO) guidelines for bicycling facilities and have been found to be less safe than on-road bike facilities.

As a result, there are no designated Bicycle Friendly Communities within Oakland County. Only the city of Novi has passed a Complete Streets resolution. Only the city of Ferndale has a comprehensive bicycle network. The city of Troy has developed the first non-motorized plan within the county but it has not been adopted by their city council (as of February 2009.)

Programs

Oakland County Community and Home Improvement Division

Funded through The Department of Housing and Urban Development (HUD) primarily in the form of Community Development Block Grants (CDBG), this program benefits low to moderate income residents of the 50 communities in Oakland County's program. CDBG funds are used to keep residential neighborhoods sound, attractive, and economically viable.

One facet of the program involves distributing low-interest, deferred-payment loans to homeowners in participating communities to update their residences. Oakland County technicians inspect approved homes and write up work specifications, which are then bid out to approximately six contractors. After bidding, homeowners may either approve the lowest bidder or pay the difference between the lowest bidder and the contractor of their choice.

Oakland County Homebuyer Program For Vacant Foreclosed Properties

Oakland County's Homebuyer Program for vacant foreclosed properties is part of the Neighborhood Stabilization Program (NSP) created by the U.S. Congress in 2008 for redeveloping and occupying abandoned and foreclosed homes. NSP is funded through The Department of Housing and Urban Development (HUD), Office of Community Planning and Development under the Community Development Block Grant (CDBG) Program and locally administered by the staff at the Oakland County Community & Home Improvement Division.

Oakland County's Homebuyer Program provides homebuyers loans for down payment assistance, closing costs, home improvements for eligible vacant foreclosed single family homes located within participating Oakland County communities.

Oakland County Main Street Program

Oakland County established the first county-level Main Street program in the U.S. in February 2000.

Main Street Oakland County (MSOC) [3] is housed within the Planning Group of the Planning & Economic Development Services Division of Oakland County's Department of Community & Economic Development. Oakland County is now a partner with the National Trust's Main Street Center [4] and contracts with them for services to the county and local communities.

MSOC ...

- empowers Oakland County's traditional downtowns to establish and/or maintain successful, comprehensive, ongoing revitalization programs;
- builds a greater awareness of the economic and quality of life importance of revitalizing and maintaining the county's historic commercial districts;
- provides the stakeholders of Oakland County's traditional downtowns with technical assistance and training resources;
- provides information about downtown revitalization to the county's communities, business organizations, and residents;

- assists communities in implementing the "Main Street Four Point Approach" to downtown management in each of the county's traditional downtowns and corridors;
- facilitates networking and communication between communities about downtown revitalization;
- provides information about county business finance programs and other economic development resources to existing downtown businesses and to those considering downtown locations;
- monitors and measures progress and success in local downtown revitalization efforts; and
- assists each of the county's 30 traditional downtowns and town centers to help them realize their full economic development potential while preserving their sense of place.

MSOC is currently working with 12 downtowns in Oakland County. These communities were selected after a detailed application process in which they demonstrated their readiness and commitment to participating in the National Trust Main Street program.

Oakland County's Main Street Communities

Farmington [5]	Keego Harbor [6]	Pontiac [7]
Ferndale [8]	Lake Orion [9]	Rochester [10]
Highland [11]	Ortonville [12]	Royal Oak [13]
Holly [14]	Oxford [15]	Walled Lake [16]

Education

Higher education

Oakland County is home to several institutions of higher education.

Baker College of Auburn Hills, located in Auburn Hills, Michigan, has a current enrollment of approximately 5,000 students. Baker College of Auburn Hills is part of the nine campus Baker College System, the largest independent college in the state of Michigan with the most focused approach to education and training available.

Oakland University, located in Rochester, is a research university with more than 18,000 students. Rated as one of the country's 82 Doctoral/Research universities by the Carnegie Foundation for the Advancement of Teaching, OU announced plans in the spring of 2007 to establish a medical school on its campus in collaboration with William Beaumont Hospital. The medical school, which will be the fourth in the state of Michigan to offer the M.D. degree, is slated to open in 2010. OU has also partnered with The Thomas M. Cooley Law School which operates one of its campuses near OU, to provide a legal curriculum.

Lawrence Technological University, located in Southfield, has a current enrollment of approximately 4,000 students. Lawrence Tech, which was originally founded in 1932 as Lawrence Institute of Technology, is consistently ranked in the top tier of Midwestern Master's Universities in the annual *U.S. News & World Report* rankings.

Rochester College, located in Rochester Hills, has a current enrollment of approximately 1,000 students. Affiliated with the Churches of Christ, Rochester College offers a variety of academic programs in the liberal arts and sciences, business, and education.

Walsh College, officially Walsh College of Accountancy and Business, has campuses in Troy, Novi, and in Macomb County.

Oakland Community College, which is one of Michigan's largest community colleges, operates five campuses throughout Oakland County: Orchard Ridge, Auburn Hills, Southfield, Highland Lakes, and Royal Oak.

Primary and secondary education

Many of the public school districts in Oakland County have multiple "National Exemplary" Schools. The International Academy (IA), which is part of the Bloomfield Hills School District, has been ranked by Newsweek as one of the top 10 public high schools in the nation every year since 2003, when IA was ranked the top public high school in the United States.

Oakland County also is home to a number of well-known private schools, including the Detroit Country Day School, Brother Rice High School, the Cranbrook Schools, Everest Academy, and the Roeper School.

Sports

Club	League	Venue	Established	Championships
Detroit Pistons	National Basketball Association	The Palace of Auburn Hills	1958 (moved to the Palace in 1988)	3
Detroit Shock	Womens National Basketball Association	Moved to Oklahoma, October 2009	1998	3
Oakland County Cruisers	FL, Baseball	Diamond at the Summit	2009	0

See also

- Saginaw Trail
- Oakland County Child Killer

External links

- Oakland County [17]
- Map of Oakland County [18]
- *An Account of Oakland County* [19] edited by Lillian Drake Avery. Dayton, Ohio: National Historical Association, Inc., [1925?]
- Clarke Historical Library, Central Michigan University, Bibliography on Oakland County [20]
- Automation Alley [21]
- Main Street Oakland County [22]
- Oakland County Home Improvement Division [23]

Geographical coordinates: 42°40′N 83°23′W

Detroit

Detroit
— City —

Top: International skyline. Middle: Woodward Avenue, Renaissance Center (General Motors World Headquarters), Lobby of the Detroit Institute of Arts Bottom: Ambassador Bridge, Old Wayne County Building, One Detroit Center

Flag

Seal

Nickname(s): The Motor City, Motown, The Renaissance City, The D, Hockeytown

Motto: "Speramus Meliora; Resurget Cineribus"
(Latin for, "We Hope For Better Things; It Shall Rise From the Ashes")

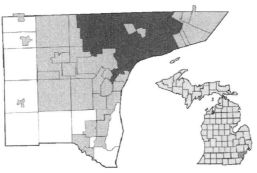

Location in Wayne County, Michigan

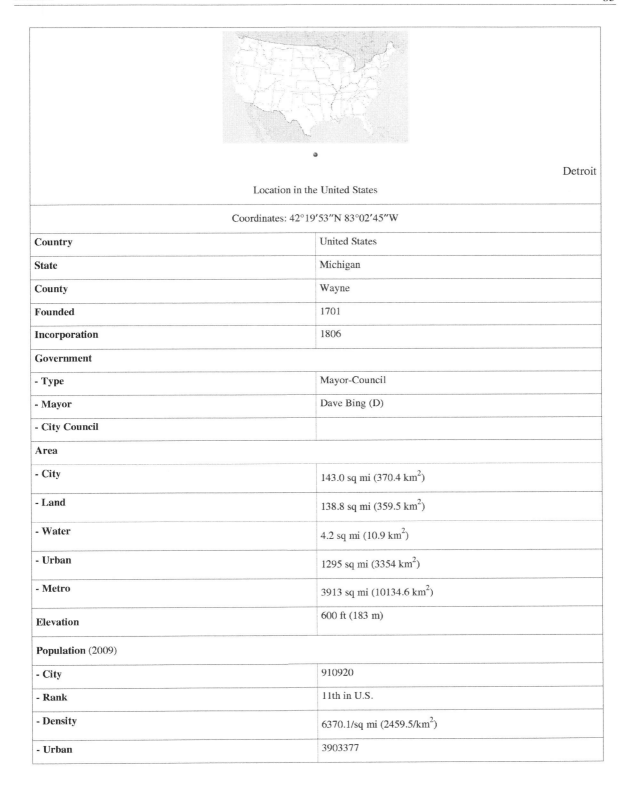

Detroit

Location in the United States

Coordinates: 42°19′53″N 83°02′45″W	
Country	United States
State	Michigan
County	Wayne
Founded	1701
Incorporation	1806
Government	
- Type	Mayor-Council
- Mayor	Dave Bing (D)
- City Council	
Area	
- City	143.0 sq mi (370.4 km^2)
- Land	138.8 sq mi (359.5 km^2)
- Water	4.2 sq mi (10.9 km^2)
- Urban	1295 sq mi (3354 km^2)
- Metro	3913 sq mi (10134.6 km^2)
Elevation	600 ft (183 m)
Population (2009)	
- City	910920
- Rank	11th in U.S.
- Density	6370.1/sq mi (2459.5/km^2)
- Urban	3903377

- Metro	4403437
- CSA	5327764
Demonym	Detroiter
Time zone	EST (UTC-5)
- Summer (DST)	EDT (UTC-4)
Area code(s)	313
FIPS code	26-22000 .
GNIS feature ID	1617959
Major airport	Detroit Metropolitan Wayne County Airport (DTW)
Website	DetroitMI.gov [1]

Detroit (pronounced /dɨˈtrɔɪt/) is the largest city in the U.S. state of Michigan and the seat of Wayne County. Detroit is a major port city on the Detroit River, in the Midwest region of the United States. Located north of Windsor, Ontario, Detroit is the only major U.S. city where Canada can be viewed by looking to the south. It was founded on July 24, 1701, by the Frenchman Antoine de la Mothe Cadillac. Its name originates from the French word *détroit* (pronounced: [detʁwa] (listen)) for strait, in reference to its location on the river connecting the Great Lakes.

Known as the world's traditional automotive center, "Detroit" is a metonym for the American automobile industry and an important source of popular music legacies celebrated by the city's two familiar nicknames, the *Motor City* and *Motown*. Other nicknames emerged in the twentieth century, including *City of Champions* beginning in the 1930s for its successes in individual and team sport, *Arsenal of Democracy* (during World War II), *The D, D-Town, Hockeytown* (a trademark owned by the city's NHL club, the Red Wings), *Rock City* (after the Kiss song "Detroit Rock City"), and *The 3-1-3* (its telephone area code).

In 2009, Detroit ranked as the United States' eleventh most populous city, with 910,920 residents. At its peak in 1950, the city was the fourth-largest in the USA, but has since seen a major shift in its population to the suburbs.

The name *Detroit* sometimes refers to the Metro Detroit area, a sprawling region with a population of 4,403,437 for the Metropolitan Statistical Area, making it the nation's eleventh-largest, and a population of 5,327,764 for the nine-county Combined Statistical Area as of the 2009 Census Bureau estimates. The Detroit–Windsor area, a critical commercial link straddling the Canada–U.S. border, has a total population of about 5,700,000.

History

Main article: History of Detroit

The city name comes from the Detroit River (French: *le détroit du Lac Érié*), meaning *the strait of Lake Erie*, linking Lake Huron and Lake Erie; in the historical context, the strait included Lake St. Clair and the St. Clair River. Traveling up the Detroit River on the ship *Le Griffon* (owned by Cavelier de La Salle), Father Louis Hennepin noted the north bank of the river as an ideal location for a settlement.

There, in 1701, the French officer Antoine de La Mothe Cadillac, along with fifty-one additional French-Canadians, founded a settlement called Fort Ponchartrain du *Détroit*, naming it after the comte de Pontchartrain, Minister of Marine under Louis XIV. France offered free land to attract families to Detroit, which grew to 800 people in 1765, the largest city between Montreal and New Orleans.

François Marie Picoté, sieur de Belestre (Montreal 1719–1793) was the last French military commander at Fort Detroit (1758–1760), surrendering the fort on November 29, 1760 to the British. The region's fur trade was an important economic activity. Detroit's city flag reflects this French heritage. (See Flag of Detroit, Michigan).

During the French and Indian War (1760), British troops gained control and shortened the name to *Detroit*. Several tribes led by Chief Pontiac, an Ottawa leader, launched Pontiac's Rebellion (1763), including a siege of Fort Detroit. Partially in response to this, the British Royal Proclamation of 1763 included restrictions on white settlement in unceded Indian territories. Detroit passed to the United States under the Jay Treaty (1796). In 1805, fire destroyed most of the settlement. A river warehouse and brick chimneys of the wooden homes were the sole structures to survive.

From 1805 to 1847, Detroit was the capital of Michigan. As the city expanded, the street layout plan developed by Augustus B. Woodward, Chief Justice of the Michigan Territory was followed. Detroit fell to British troops during the War of 1812 in the Siege of Detroit, was recaptured by the United States in 1813 and incorporated as a city in 1815.

Prior to the American Civil War, the city's access to the Canadian border made it a key stop along the underground railroad. Then a Lieutenant, the future president Ulysses S. Grant was stationed in the city. His dwelling is still at the Michigan State Fairgrounds. Because of this local sentiment, many Detroiters volunteered to fight during the American Civil War, including the 24th Michigan Infantry Regiment (part of the legendary Iron Brigade) which fought with distinction and suffered 82% casualties at Gettysburg in 1863. Abraham Lincoln is quoted as saying *Thank God for Michigan!* Following the death of President Abraham Lincoln, George Armstrong Custer delivered a eulogy to the thousands gathered near Campus Martius Park. Custer led the Michigan Brigade during the American Civil War and called them the *Wolverines*.

Corner of Michigan and Griswold, circa 1920

During the late 19th and early 20th centuries, many of the city's Gilded Age mansions and buildings arose. Detroit was referred to as the *Paris of the West* for its architecture, and for Washington Boulevard, recently electrified by Thomas Edison. Strategically located along the Great Lakes waterway, Detroit emerged as a transportation hub. The city had grown steadily from the 1830s with the rise of shipping, shipbuilding, and manufacturing industries. In 1896, a thriving carriage trade prompted Henry Ford to build his first automobile in a rented workshop on Mack Avenue.

In 1904 Ford founded the Ford Motor Company. Ford's manufacturing—and those of automotive pioneers William C. Durant, the Dodge brothers, Packard, and Walter Chrysler—reinforced Detroit's status as the world's automotive capital; it also served to encourage truck manufacturers such as Rapid and Grabowsky.

With the introduction of Prohibition, smugglers used the river as a major conduit for Canadian spirits, organized in large part by the notorious Purple Gang. Strained racial relations were evident in the 1920s trial of Dr. Ossian Sweet, a black Detroit physician acquitted of murder. A man died when shots were fired from Ossian's house into a threatening mob who gathered to try to force him out of a predominantly white neighborhood.

Cadillac Motor Co..(c.1910)
Cass Ave. at Amsterdam St.

Labor strife climaxed in the 1930s when the United Auto Workers became involved in bitter disputes with Detroit's auto manufacturers. The labor activism of those years brought notoriety to union leaders such as Jimmy Hoffa and Walter Reuther. The 1940s saw the construction of the world's first urban depressed freeway, the Davison and the industrial growth during World War II that led to Detroit's nickname as the *Arsenal of Democracy*.

Industry spurred growth during the first half of the twentieth century as the city drew tens of thousands of new residents, particularly workers from the Southern United States, to become the nation's fourth largest. At the same time, tens of thousands of European immigrants poured into the city. Social tensions rose with the rapid pace of growth. The *color blind* promotion policies of the auto plants resulted in racial tension that erupted into a full-scale riot in 1943.

Consolidation during the 1950s, especially in the automobile sector, increased competition for jobs. An extensive freeway system constructed in the 1950s and 1960s had facilitated commuting. The Twelfth Street riot in 1967, as well as court-ordered busing accelerated white flight from the city. Commensurate with the shift of population and jobs to its suburbs, the city's tax base eroded. In the years following, Detroit's population fell from a peak of roughly 1.8 million in 1950 to about half that number today.

The gasoline crises of 1973 and 1979 impacted the U.S. auto industry as small cars from foreign makers made inroads. Heroin and crack cocaine use afflicted the city with the influence of Butch Jones, Maserati Rick, and the Chambers Brothers. *Renaissance* has been a perennial buzzword among city leaders, reinforced by the construction of the Renaissance Center in the late 1970s. This complex of skyscrapers, designed as a *city within a city*, slowed but was unable to reverse the trend of businesses leaving Downtown Detroit until the 1990s.

Michigan Soldiers' and Sailors' Monument of the Civil War with the old Detroit City Hall.

In 1980, Detroit hosted the Republican National Convention which nominated Ronald Reagan to a successful bid for President of the United States. By then, nearly three decades of crime, drug addiction, and inadequate policies had caused areas like the Elmhurst block to decay. During the 1980s, abandoned structures were demolished to reduce havens for drug dealers with sizable tracts of land reverted to a form of urban prairie.

In the 1990s, the city began to receive a revival with much of it centered in the Downtown, Midtown, and New Center areas. Comerica Tower at Detroit Center (1993) arose on the city skyline. In the ensuing years, three casinos opened in Detroit: MGM Grand Detroit, MotorCity Casino, and Greektown Casino which debuted as resorts in 2007–08. New downtown stadiums were constructed for the Detroit Tigers and Detroit Lions in 2000 and 2002, respectively; this put the Lions' home stadium in the city proper for the first time since 1974.The city also saw the historic Book Cadillac Hotel and the Fort Shelby Hotel reopen for the first time in over 20 years. The city hosted the 2005 MLB All-Star Game, 2006 Super Bowl XL, 2006 World Series, WrestleMania 23 in 2007 and the NCAA Final Four in April 2009 all of which prompted many improvements to the downtown area.

The city's riverfront is the focus of much development following the example of Windsor, Ontario which began its waterfront parkland conversion in the 1990s; in 2007, the first portions of the Detroit River Walk were laid, including miles of parks and fountains. This new urban development in Detroit is a mainstay in the city's plan to enhance its economy through tourism. Along the river, developers are constructing upscale condominiums such as Watermark Detroit. Some city limit signs, particularly on the Dearborn border say "Welcome to Detroit, The Renaissance City Founded 1701."

Geography

The Detroit skyline as viewed from Malden Park in Windsor, Ontario

Topography

According to the United States Census Bureau, the city has a total area of 143.0 square miles (370 km^2); of this, 138.8 square miles (359 km^2) is land and 4.2 square miles (11 km^2) is water. Detroit is the principal city of the Metro Detroit and Southeast Michigan regions.

The highest elevation in the city is in the University District neighborhood in northwestern Detroit, west of Palmer Park, sitting at a height of 670 feet (200 m). Detroit's lowest elevation is along its riverfront, sitting at a height of 579 feet (176 m). Detroit completely encircles the cities of Hamtramck and Highland Park. On its northeast border are the communities of Grosse Pointe.

A simulated-color satellite image of the Detroit metro area, including Windsor across the river, taken on NASA's Landsat 7 satellite.

A view of the city from Belle Isle Park.

The Detroit River International Wildlife Refuge is the only international wildlife preserve in North America, uniquely located in the heart of a major metropolitan area. The Refuge includes islands, coastal wetlands, marshes, shoals, and waterfront lands along 48 miles (77 km) of the Detroit River and Western Lake Erie shoreline.

Three road systems cross the city: the original French template, radial avenues from a Washington, D.C.-inspired system, and true north–south roads from the Northwest Ordinance township system. The city is north of Windsor, Ontario. Detroit is the only major city along the U.S.–Canadian border in which one travels south in order to cross into Canada.

Detroit has four border crossings: the Ambassador Bridge and the Detroit–Windsor Tunnel provide motor vehicle thoroughfares, with the Michigan Central Railway Tunnel providing railroad access to and from Canada. The fourth border crossing is the Detroit–Windsor Truck Ferry, located near the Windsor Salt Mine and Zug Island. Near Zug Island, the southwest part of the city sits atop a 1500-acre (610 ha) salt mine that is 1100 feet (340 m) below the surface. The Detroit Salt Company mine has over 100 miles (160 km) of roads within.

Climate

Detroit and the rest of southeastern Michigan have a humid continental climate (Koppen *Dfa*) which is influenced by the Great Lakes. Winters are cold, with moderate snowfall and temperatures at night sometimes dropping below 0 °F (−17.8 °C) around 6 times per year, while summers are warm to hot with temperatures exceeding 90 °F (32.2 °C) on 12 days. Brisk winds can intensify already-cold conditions during winter and high dew points can exacerbate summer heat. Precipitation, though significant in winter, is greatest during the summer months. Snowfall, which typically occurs from November to early April, averages 43.3 inches (110 cm) per season. Monthly averages range from 24.5 °F (−4.2 °C) in January to 73.5 °F (23.1 °C) in July. The highest recorded temperature was 105 °F (40.6 °C) on July 24, 1934, while the lowest recorded temperature was −21 °F (−29.4 °C) on January 21, 1984.

Climate data for Detroit (Detroit Metro Airport)													
Month	Jan	Feb	Mar	Apr	May	Jun	Jul	Aug	Sep	Oct	Nov	Dec	Year
Record high °F (°C)	67 (19.4)	70 (21.1)	82 (27.8)	89 (31.7)	95 (35)	104 (40)	105 (40.6)	104 (40)	100 (37.8)	92 (33.3)	81 (27.2)	69 (20.6)	105 (40.6)
Average high °F (°C)	31.1 (-0.5)	34.4 (1.33)	45.2 (7.33)	57.8 (14.33)	70.2 (21.22)	79.0 (26.11)	83.4 (28.56)	81.4 (27.44)	73.7 (23.17)	61.2 (16.22)	47.8 (8.78)	35.9 (2.17)	58.4 (14.67)
Average low °F (°C)	17.8 (-7.89)	20.0 (-6.67)	28.5 (-1.94)	38.4 (3.56)	49.4 (9.67)	58.9 (14.94)	63.6 (17.56)	62.2 (16.78)	54.1 (12.28)	42.5 (5.83)	33.5 (0.83)	23.4 (-4.78)	41.0 (5)
Record low °F (°C)	−21	−20	−4	8 (-13.3)	26 (-3.3)	36 (2.2)	42 (5.6)	38 (3.3)	29 (-1.7)	17 (-8.3)	0 (-17.8)	−11	−21
Precipitation inches (mm)	1.91 (48.5)	1.88 (47.8)	2.52 (64)	3.05 (77.5)	3.05 (77.5)	3.55 (90.2)	3.16 (80.3)	3.10 (78.7)	3.27 (83.1)	2.23 (56.6)	2.66 (67.6)	2.51 (63.8)	32.89 (835.4)
Snowfall inches (cm)	11.3 (28.7)	9.2 (23.4)	6.8 (17.3)	1.7 (4.3)	0 (0)	0 (0)	0 (0)	0 (0)	0 (0)	.3 (0.8)	2.9 (7.4)	11.1 (28.2)	43.3 (110)
Avg. precipitation days (≥ 0.01 in)	13.4	11.3	12.7	12.6	11.6	10.1	9.6	9.5	9.9	9.8	12.3	13.9	136.7
Avg. snowy days (≥ 0.1 in)	10.9	7.9	5.5	2.1	0	0	0	0	0	.3	3.5	9.0	39.2
Sunshine hours	120.9	138.4	186.0	216.0	275.9	303.0	316.2	282.1	228.0	176.7	105.0	86.8	2435
Source #1: NOAA (normals 1971–2000, records 1874–2009)													
Source #2: HKO (sun, 1961–1990)													

Cityscape

Detroit International Riverfront

Architecture

Main article: Architecture of metropolitan Detroit

Cadillac Place (1923) left, with the Fisher Building (1928) are among the city's National Historic Landmarks.

Seen in panorama, Detroit's waterfront shows a variety of architectural styles. The post modern neogothic spires of the Comerica Tower at Detroit Center (1993) were designed to blend with the city's Art Deco skyscrapers. Together with the Renaissance Center, they form a distinctive and recognizable skyline. Examples of the Art Deco style include the Guardian Building and Penobscot Building downtown, as well as the Fisher Building and Cadillac Place in the New Center area near Wayne State University. Among the city's prominent structures are the nation's largest Fox Theatre, the Detroit Opera House, and the Detroit Institute of Arts.

While the downtown and New Center areas contain high-rise buildings, the majority of the surrounding city consists of low-rise structures and single-family homes. Outside of the city's core, residential high-rises are found in neighborhoods such as the East Riverfront extending toward Grosse Pointe and the Palmer Park neighborhood just west of Woodward.

Neighborhoods constructed prior to World War II feature the architecture of the times with wood frame and brick houses in the working class neighborhoods, larger brick homes in middle class neighborhoods, and ornate mansions in neighborhoods such as Brush Park, Woodbridge, Indian Village, Palmer Woods, Boston-Edison, and others.

St. Joseph Catholic Church (1873) is
a notable example of Detroit's
ecclesial architecture.

The oldest neighborhoods are along the Woodward and East Jefferson corridors, while neighborhoods built in the 1950s are found in the far west and closer to 8 Mile Road. Some of the oldest extant neighborhoods include Corktown, a working class, formerly Irish neighborhood, and Brush Park. Both are now seeing multi-million dollar restorations and construction of new homes and condominiums.

Many of the city's architecturally significant buildings are on the National Register of Historic Places and the city has one of the nation's largest surviving collections of late 19th and early 20th century buildings. There are a number of architecturally significant churches, including St. Joseph Catholic Church, St. Mary Catholic Church, and Ste. Anne de Detroit Catholic Church.

There is substantial activity in urban design, historic preservation and architecture. A number of downtown redevelopment projects—of which Campus Martius Park is one of the most notable—have revitalized parts of the city. Grand Circus Park stands near the city's theater district, Ford Field, home of the Detroit Lions, and Comerica Park, home of the Detroit Tigers.

Detroit Financial District viewed
from the International Riverfront.

The Detroit International Riverfront includes a partially completed three and one-half mile riverfront promenade with a combination of parks, residential buildings, and commercial areas from Hart Plaza to the MacArthur Bridge accessing Belle Isle (the largest island park in a U.S. city). The riverfront includes Tri-Centennial State Park and Harbor, Michigan's first urban state park. The second phase is a two mile (3 km) extension from Hart Plaza to the Ambassador Bridge for a total of five miles (8 km) of parkway from bridge to bridge. Civic planners envision that the riverfront properties condemned under eminent domain, with their pedestrian parks, will spur more residential development. Other major parks include Palmer (north of Highland Park), River Rouge (in the southwest side), and Chene Park (on the east river downtown).

Neighborhoods

Further information: Neighborhoods in Detroit, Urban development in Detroit, and Public housing in Detroit

Detroit has a variety of neighborhood types. The revitalized Downtown, Midtown, and New Center areas feature many historic buildings and are high density, while further out, particularly in the northeast and on the fringes, the city suffers from severe vacancy issues, for which a number of solutions have been proposed.

The National Register of Historic Places lists several area neighborhoods and districts such as Lafayette Park, part of the Ludwig Mies van der Rohe residential district. Lafayette Park is a revitalized neighorhood on the city's east side. The 78-acre (32 ha) urban renewal project was originally called the Gratiot Park Development. Planned by Mies van der Rohe, Ludwig Hilberseimer and Alfred Caldwell it includes a landscaped, 19-acre (7.7 ha) park with no through traffic, in which these and other low-rise apartment buildings are situated.

Eastern Market.

On Saturdays, about 45,000 people shop the city's historic Eastern Market. The Midtown and the New Center area are centered on Wayne State University and Henry Ford Hospital. Midtown has about 50,000 residents and attracts millions of visitors each year to its museums and cultural centers; for example, the Detroit Festival of the Arts in Midtown draws about 350,000 people.

The University Commons-Palmer Park district in northwest Detroit is near the University of Detroit Mercy and Marygrove College which anchors historic neighborhoods including Palmer Woods, Sherwood Forest, Green Acres, and the University District. In 2007, Downtown Detroit was named 18th (out of 35) best neighborhood in which to retire among the nation's 30 largest metro areas by CNN Money Magazine editors.

Detroit has numerous neighborhoods suffering from urban decay, consisting of vacant properties.

These neighborhoods are concentrated in the northeast and on the city's fringes. The 2009 residential lot vacancy in Detroit was 27.8%, up from 10.3% in 2000, with the population continuing to shrink and foreclosures that exacerbate the problem. An estimated 20 to 30 percent of lots are vacant. A 2009 parcel survey found 33,527 or 10% of the city's housing to be unoccupied, but recommended that only one percent or 3,480 of the city's housing units be demolished. The city states it costs about $10,000 to demolish one vacant house, which takes many legal steps. In 2010, the city began using federal funds on its quest to demolish 10,000 empty residential structures. About 3,000 of these of the residential structures will be torn down in 2010. A number of solutions have been proposed for dealing with the shrinkage, including resident relocation from more sparsely populated neighborhoods and converting unused space to agricultural use, though the city expects to be in the planning stages for up to another two years. In April 2008, the city announced a $300-million stimulus plan to create jobs and revitalize neighborhoods, financed by city bonds and paid for by earmarking about 15% of the wagering tax. The city's working plans for neighborhood revitalizations include 7-Mile/Livernois, Brightmoor, East English Village, Grand River/Greenfield, North-End, and Osborn. Private organizations have pledged substantial funding to the efforts.

Immigrants have contributed to the city's neighborhood revitalization, especially in southwest Detroit. Southwest Detroit has experienced a thriving economy in recent years, as evidenced by new housing, increased business openings and the recently opened Mexicantown International Welcome Center.

Culture and contemporary life

Downtown Detroit is growing in its population of young professionals and retail is expanding. A number of luxury high rises have been built. The east river development plans include more luxury condominium developments. A desire to be closer to the urban scene has attracted young professionals to take up residence among the mansions of Grosse Pointe just outside the city. Detroit's proximity to Windsor, Ontario, provides for views and nightlife, along with Ontario's minimum drinking age of 19.

Entertainment and performing arts

Main articles: Culture of Detroit, Music of Detroit, Theatre in Detroit, and Detroit celebrities

Fox Theatre lights up 'Foxtown' in downtown Detroit

Live music has been a prominent feature of Detroit's nightlife since the late 1940s, bringing the city recognition under the nickname Motown. The metropolitan area has many nationally prominent live music venues. Concerts hosted by Live Nation perform throughout the Detroit area. Large concerts are held at DTE Energy Music Theatre and The Palace of Auburn Hills. The Detroit Theatre District is the nation's second largest and hosts Broadway performances. Major theaters include the Fox Theatre, Music Hall, the Gem Theatre, Masonic Temple Theatre, the Detroit Opera House, the Fisher Theatre and Orchestra Hall which hosts the renowned Detroit Symphony Orchestra. The Nederlander Organization, the largest controller of Broadway productions in New York City, originated with the purchase of the Detroit Opera House in 1922 by the Nederlander family.

Movie studios are planned for the metro area. Motown Motion Picture Studios with 600000 square feet (56000 m^2) will produce movies in Detroit and the surrounding area based at the Pontiac Centerpoint Business Campus for a film industry expected to employ over 4,000 people in the metro area.

Important music events in the city include: the Detroit International Jazz Festival, the Detroit Electronic Music Festival, the Motor City Music Conference (MC2), the Urban Organic Music Conference, the Concert of Colors, and the hip-hop Summer Jamz festival.

The city of Detroit has a rich musical heritage and has contributed to a number of different genres over the decades leading into the new millennium.

In the 1940s, blues artist John Lee Hooker became a long-term resident in the city's southwest Delray neighborhood. Hooker, among other important blues musicians migrated from his home in Mississippi bringing the Delta Blues to northern cities like Detroit. Hooker recorded for Fortune Records, the biggest pre-Motown blues/soul label. During the 1950s, the city became a center for jazz, with stars performing in the Black Bottom neighborhood. Prominent emerging Jazz musicians of the 1960s included: trumpet player Donald Byrd who attended Cass Tech and performed with Art Blakey and the Jazz Messengers early in his career and Saxophonist Pepper Adams who enjoyed a solo career and accompanied Byrd on several albums. The Graystone International Jazz Museum documents jazz in Detroit.

Other, prominent Motor City R&B stars in the 1950s and early 1960s was Nolan Strong, Andre Williams and Nathaniel Mayer - who all scored local and national hits on the Fortune Records label. According to Smokey Robinson, Strong was a primary influence on his voice as a teenager. The Fortune label was a family-operated label located on Third Avenue in Detroit, and was owned by the husband and wife team of Jack Brown and Devora Brown. Fortune, which also released country, gospel and rockabilly LPs and 45s, laid the groundwork for Motown, which became Detroit's most legendary record label.

Berry Gordy, Jr. founded Motown Records which rose to prominence during the 1960s and early 1970s with acts such as Stevie Wonder, The Temptations, The Four Tops, Smokey Robinson & The Miracles, Diana Ross & The Supremes, the Jackson 5, Martha and the Vandellas and Marvin Gaye. The Motown Sound played an important role in the crossover appeal with popular music, since it was the first African American owned record label to primarily feature African-American artists. Gordy moved Motown to Los Angeles in 1972 to pursue film production, but the company has since returned to Detroit.

MGM Grand Detroit.

Aretha Franklin, another Detroit R&B star, carried the Motown Sound; however, she did not record with Berry's Motown Label.

Local artists and bands rose to prominence in the 1960s and 70s including: the MC5, The Stooges, Bob Seger, Amboy Dukes featuring Ted Nugent, Mitch Ryder and The Detroit Wheels, Rare Earth, Alice Cooper, and Suzi Quatro. The group Kiss emphasized the city's connection with rock in the song *Detroit Rock City* and the movie produced in 1999. In the 1980s, Detroit was an important center of the hardcore punk rock underground with many nationally known bands coming out of the city and its suburbs, such as The Necros, The Meatmen, and Negative Approach.

In 1990s and the new millennium, the city has produced a number of influential artists, for example Eminem, the hip-hop artist with the highest cumulative sales, and hip hop producer J Dilla. Detroit is cited as the birthplace of techno music. Prominent Detroit Techno artists include Juan Atkins, Derrick May, and Kevin Saunderson. The band Sponge toured and produced music, with artists such as Kid Rock and Uncle Kracker. The city has an active garage rock genre that has generated national attention with acts such as: The White Stripes, The Von Bondies, The Dirtbombs, Electric Six, and The Hard Lessons.

Tourism

Main article: Tourism in metropolitan Detroit

Many of the area's prominent museums are located in the historic cultural center neighborhood around Wayne State University. These museums include the Detroit Institute of Arts, the Detroit Historical Museum, Charles H. Wright Museum of African American History, the

Detroit Institute of Arts

Detroit Science Center, and the main branch of the Detroit Public Library. Other cultural highlights include Motown Historical Museum, Tuskegee Airmen Museum, Fort Wayne, Dossin Great Lakes Museum, the Museum of Contemporary Art Detroit (MOCAD), the Contemporary Art Institute of Detroit (CAID), and the Belle Isle Conservatory. Important history of Detroit and the surrounding area is exhibited at The Henry Ford, the nation's largest indoor-outdoor museum complex. The Detroit Historical Society provides information about tours of area churches, skyscrapers, and mansions. The Eastern Market farmer's distribution center is the largest open-air flowerbed market in the United States and has more than 150 foods and specialty businesses. Other sites of interest are the Detroit Zoo and the Anna Scripps Whitcomb Conservatory on Belle Isle.

The city's Greektown and casino resorts serve as an entertainment hub. Annual summer events include the Detroit Electronic Music Festival, Detroit International Jazz Festival, and Woodward Dream Cruise. Within downtown, Campus Martius Park hosts large events such as the Motown Winter Blast. As the world's traditional automotive center, the city hosts the North American International Auto

Show. Held since 1924, America's Thanksgiving Parade is one of the nation's largest. The Motown Winter Blast, and the summer River Days, a five-day festival on the International Riverfront, leading up to the Windsor-Detroit International Freedom Festival fireworks can draw super sized-crowds of hundreds of thousands to over three million people.

An important civic sculpture in Detroit is Marshall Fredericks' "Spirit of Detroit" at the Coleman Young Municipal Center. The image is often used as a symbol of Detroit and the statue itself is occasionally dressed in sports jerseys to celebrate when a Detroit team is doing well. A memorial to Joe Louis at the intersection of Jefferson and Woodward Avenues was dedicated on October 16, 1986. The sculpture, commissioned by *Sports Illustrated* and executed by Robert Graham, is a twenty-four foot (7.3 m) long arm with a fisted hand suspended by a pyramidal framework.

Artist Tyree Guyton created the controversial street art exhibit known as the Heidelberg Project in the mid 1980s, using found objects including cars, clothing and shoes found in the neighborhood near and on Heidelberg Street on the near East Side of Detroit.

Sports

Further information: Sports in Detroit and U.S. cities with teams from four major sports

Detroit is one of 13 American metropolitan areas that are home to professional teams representing the four major sports in North America. All these teams but one play within the city of Detroit itself (the NBA's Detroit Pistons play in suburban Auburn Hills at The Palace of Auburn Hills). There are three active major sports venues within the city: Comerica Park (home of the Major League Baseball team Detroit Tigers), Ford Field (home of the NFL's Detroit Lions), and Joe Louis Arena (home of the NHL's Detroit Red Wings). A 1996 marketing campaign promoted the nickname "Hockeytown".

Looking towards Ford Field the night of Super Bowl XL.

In college sports, Detroit's central location within the Mid-American Conference has made it a frequent site for the league's championship events. While the MAC Basketball Tournament moved permanently to Cleveland starting in 2000, the MAC Football Championship Game has been played at Ford Field in Detroit since 2004, and annually attracts 25,000 to 30,000 fans. The University of Detroit Mercy has a NCAA Division I program, and Wayne State University has both NCAA Division I and II programs. The NCAA football Little Caesars Pizza Bowl is held at Ford Field each December.

Sailboat racing is a major sport in the Detroit area. Lake Saint Clair is home to many yacht clubs which host regattas. Bayview Yacht Club, the Detroit Yacht Club, Crescent Sail Yacht Club, Grosse Pointe Yacht Club, The Windsor Yacht Club, and the Edison Boat Club each participate in and are governed by the Detroit Regional Yacht-Racing Association or DRYA. Detroit is home to many One-Design fleets including, but not limited to, North American 40s, Cal 25s, Cuthbertson and Cassian 35s, Crescent Sailboats, Express 27s, J 120s, J 105, Flying Scots, and many more.

The Crescent Sailboat, NA-40, and the L boat were designed and built exclusively in Detroit. Detroit also has a very active and competitive junior sailing program. The junior sailing program at the Grosse Pointe Yacht Club is renowned for producing world class sailors such as Carrie Howe and Jack Wheeler.

Comerica Park 2007

Since 1916, the city has been home to an Unlimited hydroplane boat race, held annually (with exceptions) on the Detroit River near Belle Isle. Often, the race is for the APBA Challenge Cup, more commonly known as the Gold Cup (first awarded in 1904, created by Tiffany) which is the oldest active motorsport trophy in the world.

Detroit is the former home of a round of the Formula One World Championship, which organized the race on the streets of downtown Detroit from 1982 until 1988, after which the sanction moved from Formula One to IndyCars until its final run in 2001. In 2007, open-wheel racing returned to Belle Isle with both Indy Racing League and American Le Mans Series Racing.

In the years following the mid-1930s, Detroit was referred to as the "City of Champions" after the Tigers, Lions, and Red Wings captured all 3 major professional sports championships in a 7 month period of time (the Tigers won the World Series in October, 1935; the Lions won the NFL championship in December, 1935; the Red Wings won the Stanley Cup in April, 1936). Gar Wood (a native Detroiter) won the Harmsworth Trophy for unlimited powerboat racing on the Detroit River in 1931. In the next year, 1932, Eddie "The Midnight Express" Tolan, a black student from Detroit's Cass Technical High School, won the 100- and 200-meter races and two gold medals at the 1932 Summer Olympics. Joe Louis won the heavyweight championship of the world in 1937. Also, in 1935 the Detroit Lions won the NFL championship. The Detroit Tigers have won ten American League pennants (The most recent being in 2006) and four World Series titles. In 1984, the Detroit Tigers' World Series championship, after which crowds had left three dead and millions of dollars in property damage. The Detroit Red Wings have won 11 Stanley Cups (the most by an American NHL Franchise), the Detroit Pistons have won three NBA titles, and the Detroit Shock have won three WNBA titles. In 2007, Detroit was given the nickname "Sports City USA" in recognition of its numerous sports teams with good game statistics and the high amount of dedicated sports fans.

Detroit has the distinction of being the city which has made the most bids to host the Summer Olympics without ever being awarded the games: seven unsuccessful bids for the 1944, 1952, 1956, 1960, 1964, 1968 and 1972 games. It came as high as second place in the balloting two times, losing the 1964 games to Tokyo and the 1968 games to Mexico City.

Detroit hosts many WWE events such as the 2007 WWE's WrestleMania 23 which attracted 80,103 fans to Ford Field; the event marking the 20th anniversary of WrestleMania III which drew a reported 93,173 to the Pontiac Silverdome in nearby Pontiac, Michigan in 1987.

On May 31 and June 1 of 2008, The Red Bull Air Race took place along the Detroit River.

Media

Main article: Media in Detroit

The *Detroit Free Press* and *The Detroit News* are the major daily newspapers, both broadsheet publications published together under a joint operating agreement. Media philanthropy includes the *Detroit Free Press* high school journalism program and the Old Newsboys' Goodfellow Fund of Detroit. In December, 2008, the Detroit Media Partnership announced that the two papers would reduce home delivery to three days a week, print reduced newsstand issues of the papers on non-delivery days and focus resources on Internet-based news delivery. These changes went into effect in March, 2009. Founded in 1980, the Metro Times is the city's alternative news weekly, covering news, arts & entertainment.

The Detroit television market is the eleventh largest in the United States; according to estimates that do not include audiences located in large areas of Ontario, Canada (Windsor and its surrounding area on broadcast and cable, as well as several other cable markets in Ontario, such as the city of Ottawa) which receive and watch Detroit television stations.

Detroit has the eleventh largest radio market in the United States, though this ranking does not take into account Canadian audiences.

Economy

Main article: Economy of metropolitan Detroit

The Renaissance Center is the world
headquarters of General Motors.

Detroit and the surrounding region constitute a major manufacturing center, most notably as home to the Big Three automobile companies, General Motors, Ford, and Chrysler. The city is an important center for global trade with large international law firms having their offices in both Detroit and Windsor. About 80,500 people work in downtown Detroit, comprising 21% of the City's employment.

There are about four thousand factories in the area. The domestic auto industry is primarily headquartered in Metro Detroit. New vehicle production, sales, and jobs related to automobile use account for one of every ten jobs in the United States. The area is also an important source of engineering job opportunities. A 2004 Border Transportation Partnership study showed that 150,000 jobs in the Windsor-Detroit region and $13 billion in annual production depend on the City of Detroit's international border crossing.

The Detroit area is accustomed to the economic cycles of the auto industry. A rise in automated manufacturing using robotic technology has created related industries in the area; inexpensive labor in other parts of the world and increased competition have led to a steady transformation of certain types of manufacturing jobs in the region with the Detroit area gaining new lithium ion battery plants. Local complications for the city include higher taxes than the nearby suburbs, with many unable to afford the levies on property. In addition to property taxes, residents must pay an income tax rate of 2.50%. In January 2010, the Department of Labor reported metropolitan Detroit's unemployment rate rose to 15.3%. Since 2009, the area's total employment contracted 1.7%. The Labor Department reported at 24.3% for December 2009.

The city has cleared large swaths of land while retaining a number of historically significant vacant buildings in order to spur redevelopment; though the city has struggled with finances, it issued bonds in 2008 to provide funding for ongoing work to demolish blighted properties. In 2006, downtown Detroit reported $1.3 billion in restorations and new developments which increased the number of construction jobs in the city. In decade leading up to 2006, downtown Detroit gained more than $15 billion in new investment from private and public sectors.

The Detroit automakers and local manufacturing have taken heavy hits as a result of market competition from foreign rivals. The 2000s energy crisis, the subsequent Late-2000s recession, and the increasingly unwieldy burden of employee retirement and healthcare costs have all been implicated. Concern among analysts over restored profits has fueled economic uncertainty in the metro Detroit area.

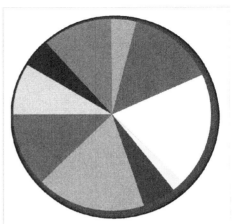

Labor force distribution in Detroit by category: Construction   Manufacturing   Trade, transportation, utilities   Information   Finance   Professional and business services   Education and health services   Leisure and hospitality   Other services   Government

In January 2009, President Barack Obama formed an automotive task force in order to help the industry recover. The severity of the recession required Detroit's automakers to take additional steps to restructure, including idling many plants. With the U.S. Treasury extending the necessary debtor in possession financing, Chrysler and GM emerged from 'pre-packaged' Chapter 11 reorganizations in June and July 2009 respectively.

GM plans to issue an initial public offering (IPO) of stock in 2010. General Motors has invested heavily in all fuel cell equipped vehicles, while Chrysler is focusing much of its research and development into biodiesel. In August 2009, Michigan and Detroit's auto industry received $1.36 B in grants from the U.S. Department of Energy for the manufacture of lithium-ion batteries.

Firms in the region pursue emerging technologies including biotechnology, nanotechnology, information technology, and hydrogen fuel cell development. The city of Detroit has made efforts to lure the region's growth companies downtown with advantages such as a wireless Internet zone, business tax incentives, entertainment, an international riverfront, and residential high rises. Thus far, the city has had some success, most notably the addition of Compuware World Headquarters, OnStar, regional offices of HP Enterprise Services at Tower 500 of the Renaissance Center, PricewaterhouseCoopers Plaza offices adjacent to Ford Field, and the 2006 completion of Ernst & Young's offices at One Kennedy Square.

Compuware World Headquarters viewed from
Bagley Memorial Fountain on Cadillac Square.

On November 12, 2007, Quicken Loans announced its development agreement with the city to move its world headquarters, and 4,000 employees, to downtown Detroit, consolidating its suburban offices, a move considered to be a high importance to city planners to reestablish the historic downtown. The construction sites reserved for development by the agreement include the location of the former Statler on Grand Circus Park and the former Hudson's location. Some Fortune 500 companies headquartered in Detroit include General Motors, auto parts maker American Axle & Manufacturing, and DTE Energy. Other major industries include advertising, law, finance, chemicals, and computer software. Medical service providers such as the Detroit Medical Center and Henry Ford Hospital are major employers in the city.

Casino gaming plays an important economic role, with Detroit the largest city in the United States to offer casino resorts. Caesars Windsor, Canada's largest, complements the MGM Grand Detroit, MotorCity Casino, and Greektown Casino in Detroit. Though the casinos have brought new tax revenue and jobs to the city, the city still has high unemployment. Gaming revenues have grown steadily, with Detroit ranked as the fifth largest gambling market in the USA for 2007. When Casino Windsor is included, Detroit's gambling market ranks third or fourth. In an effort to support spending within the city, certain business owners set up "mints" to distribute the Detroit Community Scrip. The scrip is used at local clubs and bars to ensure some dollars stay within the city by establishing a note that is only legal tender at certain places.

Demographics

See also: Demographic profile of Detroit

In 2009, Detroit ranked as the United States' eleventh most populous city, with 910,920 residents. The name *Detroit* sometimes refers to Metro Detroit, a six-county area with a population of 4,403,437 for the Metropolitan Statistical Area, making it the nation's eleventh-largest, and a population of 5,327,764 for the nine-county Combined Statistical Area as of the 2009 Census Bureau estimates. The Detroit-Windsor area, a critical commercial link straddling the Canada-U.S. border, has a total population of about 5,700,000. Immigration continues to play a role in the region's projected growth.

Historical populations			
Census	City	Metro	Region
1820	1,422	N/A	N/A
1830	2,222	N/A	N/A
1840	9,102	N/A	N/A
1850	21,019	N/A	N/A
1860	45,619	N/A	N/A
1870	79,577	N/A	N/A
1880	116,340	N/A	N/A
1890	205,877	N/A	N/A
1900	285,704	542,452	664,771
1910	465,766	725,064	867,250
1920	993,678	1,426,704	1,639,006
1930	1,568,662	2,325,739	2,655,395
1940	1,623,452	2,544,287	2,911,681
1950	1,849,568	3,219,256	3,700,490
1960	1,670,144	4,012,607	4,660,480
1970	1,514,063	4,490,902	5,289,766
1980	1,203,368	4,387,783	5,203,269
1990	1,027,974	4,266,654	5,095,695
2000	951,270	4,441,551	5,357,538
2009*	910,920	4,403,437	5,327,764

*Estimates Metro: Metropolitan Statistical Area (MSA)

Region: Combined Statistical Area (CSA)

Detroit had 33.8% of its residents below the poverty level in 2007, the highest among large U.S. cities. This stands in stark contrast to Metro Detroit suburbs, which are among the more affluent in the U.S.

The city's population increased more than sixfold during the first half of the twentieth century, fed largely by an influx of European, Middle Eastern (Lebanese),(Assyrian/Chaldean), and Southern migrants to work in the burgeoning automobile industry. However, since 1950 the city has seen a major shift in its population to the suburbs. In 1910, fewer than 6,000 blacks called the city home; in 1930 more than 120,000 blacks lived in Detroit. The thousands of African Americans who came to Detroit were part of the Great Migration of the 20th century.

The city population dropped from its peak in 1950 with a population of 1,849,568 to 910,920 in 2009. This is partly attributable to the construction of an extensive freeway system during the 1950s and white flight, while many residents have relocated to the Sun belt. In the 2000s, 70% of the total black population in Metro Detroit lived in the City of Detroit.

As of the 2000 Census, there were 951,270 people, 336,428 households, and 218,341 families residing in the city. The population density was 6,855.1 people per square mile (2,646.7/km²). There were 375,096 housing units at an average density of 2,703.0 units per square mile (1,043.6/km²). The racial makeup of the city was 81.6% Black, 12.3% White, 1.0% Asian, 0.3% Native American, 0.03% Pacific Islander, 2.5% other races, 2.3% two or more races, and 5.0 percent Hispanic (mostly Puerto Rican and Mexican). The city's foreign-born population is at 4.8%. Estimates from the 2006–2008 American Community Survey showed little variance.

There were 336,428 households out of which 33.9% have children under the age of 18 living with them, 26.7% were married couples living together, 31.6% had a female householder with no husband present, and 35.1% were non-families, 29.7% of all households were made up of individuals and 9.2% had someone living alone who is 65 years of age or older. The average household size was 2.77 and the average family size was 3.45.

There is a wide age distribution in the city, with 31.1% under the age of 18, 9.7% from 18 to 24, 29.5% from 25 to 44, 19.3% from 45 to 64, and 10.4% who are 65 years of age or older. The median age was 31 years. For every 100 females there were 89.1 males. For every 100 females age 18 and over, there were 83.5 males.

For the 2000 Census, median household income in the city was $29,526, and the median income for a family was $33,853. Males had a median income of $33,381 versus $26,749 for females. The per capita income for the city was $14,717. 26.1% of the population and 21.7% of families were below the poverty line. Out of the total population, 34.5% of those under the age of 18 and 18.6% of those 65 and older were living below the poverty line.

A 2007 Social Compact report showed the city of Detroit's median household income at $34,512, a 12% increase over the Census estimate. The 2008 Census estimate placed the median household income $28,730, a 2.7% increase from 2000.

Law and government

Further information: Government of Detroit and List of mayors of Detroit

The city government is run by a mayor and nine-member city council and clerk elected on an at-large nonpartisan ballot. Since voters approved the city's charter in 1974, Detroit has had a "strong mayoral" system, with the mayor approving departmental appointments. The council approves budgets but the mayor is not obligated to adhere to any earmarking. City ordinances and substantially large contracts must be approved by the council. The city clerk supervises elections and is formally charged with the maintenance of municipal records. Municipal elections for mayor, city council and city clerk are held at four-year intervals, in the year after presidential elections (so that there are Detroit elections scheduled in 1993, 1997, 2001, 2005, 2009, etc.). Following a November 2009 referendum, seven council members will be elected from districts beginning in 2013 while two will continue to be elected at-large.

The historic Guardian Building is Wayne County, MichiganWayne County headquarters.

Detroit's courts are state-administered and elections are nonpartisan.
The Probate Court for Wayne County is located in the Coleman A. Young Municipal Center in downtown Detroit. The Circuit Court is located across Gratiot Ave. in the Frank Murphy Hall of Justice, in downtown Detroit. The city is home to the Thirty Sixth District Court, as well as the First District of the Michigan Court of Appeals and the United States District Court for the Eastern District of Michigan.

Detroit has several sister cities, including Chongqing (People's Republic of China), Dubai (United Arab Emirates), Kitwe (Zambia), Minsk (Belarus), Nassau, Bahamas, Toyota (Japan), and Turin (Italy).

Politics

Politically, the city consistently supports the Democratic Party in state and national elections (local elections are nonpartisan). According to a study released by the Bay Area Center for Voting Research, Detroit is the most liberal large city in America, measuring only the percentage of city residents who voted for the Democratic Party.

In 2000, the City requested an investigation by the United States Justice Department into the Detroit Police Department which was concluded in 2003 over allegations regarding its use of force and civil rights violations. The city proceeded with a major reorganization of the Detroit Police Department.

Urban development in Detroit has been an important issue. In 1973, the city elected its first black mayor, Coleman Young. Despite development efforts, his combative style during his five terms in office was not well received by many whites. Mayor Dennis Archer, a former Michigan Supreme Court Justice, refocused the city's attention on redevelopment with a plan to permit three casinos downtown.

Mayor Kwame Kilpatrick resigned his office effective September 19, 2008, after pleading guilty to two counts of obstruction of justice and no contest to one count of assaulting and obstructing a police officer. Kilpatrick was succeeded in office on an interim basis by City Council President Kenneth Cockrel, Jr. until a May, 2009 special election in which businessman and former Detroit Pistons star Dave Bing was elected Mayor for the remaining duration of Kilpatrick's term. Bing has since been re-elected to his first full term of office, and is Detroit's current mayor.

Crime

Main article: Crime in Detroit

Although crime has declined significantly since the 1970s, the violent crime rate is one of the highest in the nation, while the chances are roughly 1 in 16 to be a victim of a property crime. The city had the sixth highest number of violent crimes among the twenty-five largest US cities in 2007. The rate of violent crime dropped 11 percent in 2008, though Wayne County Prosecutor questions the finding. The decline follows a national trend, while Police Commissioner William Dwyer implicates stepped up police initiatives for the drop. Neighborhoodscout.com reported a crime rate of 62.18 per 1000 residents for property crimes, and 16.73 per 1000 for violent crimes (compared to national figures of 32 per 1000 for property crimes and 5 per 1000 for violent crime in 2008)

The city's downtown is far safer by comparison with a 2006 study showing crime in downtown Detroit to be much lower than national, state and metro averages. According to a 2007 analysis, Detroit officials note that about 65 to 70 percent of homicides in the city were drug related.

Education

Colleges and universities

See also: Colleges and universities in Metro Detroit

Detroit is home to several institutions of higher learning, including Wayne State University, a national research university with medical and law schools in the Midtown area. Other institutions in the city include the University of Detroit Mercy with its schools of Law, Dentistry, and Nursing, the College for Creative Studies, Lewis College of Business, Marygrove College and Wayne County Community College. In June 2009 the Michigan State University College of Osteopathic Medicine will be opening a satellite campus located at the Detroit Medical Center. The Detroit College of Law, now affiliated with Michigan State University, was founded in the city in 1891 and remained there until 1997, when it relocated to East Lansing. The University of Michigan was established in 1817 in Detroit and later moved to Ann Arbor in 1837. In 1959, University of Michigan–Dearborn was established in neighboring Dearborn.

Old Main, a historic building at Wayne State University.

Primary and secondary schools

WWI Memorial Clock Tower at University of Detroit Mercy.

Public schools and charter schools

With about 84,000 public school students (2010–11), the Detroit Public Schools (DPS) district is the largest school district in Michigan. Detroit has an additional 54,000 charter school students for a combined enrollment of about 138,000 students.

In the mid- to late 1990s, the Michigan Legislature removed the locally elected board of education amid

Detroit Public Library.

allegations of mismanagement and replaced it with a reform board appointed by the mayor and governor. The elected board of education was re-established following a city referendum in 2005. The first election of the new eleven-member board of education occurred on November 8, 2005. Due to growing Detroit Charter Schools enrollment, the city planned to close many public schools. State officials report a 68% graduation rate for Detroit's public schools adjusted for those who change schools.

Private schools

Detroit is served by various private schools, as well as parochial Roman Catholic schools operated by the Archdiocese of Detroit. The Archdiocese of Detroit lists a number of primary and secondary schools in the city, along with those in the metro area, but Catholic education has contracted from its earlier base in the city and emigrated to the suburbs. There are 23 Catholic high schools in the Archdiocese of Detroit. Of the three Catholic high schools in the city, two are operated by the Society of Jesus and the third is co-sponsored by the Sisters, Servants of the Immaculate Heart of Mary and the Congregation of St. Basil.

Infrastructure

Health systems

Within the city of Detroit, there are over a dozen major hospitals which include the Detroit Medical Center (DMC), Henry Ford Health System, St. John Health System, and the John D. Dingell VA Medical Center. The DMC, a regional Level I trauma center, consists of Detroit Receiving Hospital and University Health Center, Children's Hospital of Michigan, Harper University Hospital, Hutzel Women's Hospital, Rehabilitation Institute of Michigan, Sinai-Grace Hospital, and the Karmanos Cancer Institute. The DMC has more than 2,000 licensed beds and 3,000 affiliated physicians. It is the largest private employer in the City of Detroit. The center is staffed by physicians from the Wayne State University School of Medicine, the largest single-campus medical school in the United States, and the nation's fourth largest medical school overall. On March 19, 2010, Vanguard Health Systems announced plans to invest nearly $1.5 B in Detroit Medical Center, including $850 M for expansion and renovation, and $417 M to retire debts, pending approval of its acquisition. In 2010, Henry Ford Health System in the New Center also announced a $500 M expansion in Detroit with plans for a biomedical research center. The metro area has many other hospitals, among which are William Beaumont Hospital, St. Joseph's, and University of Michigan Medical Center, mostly in suburban counties.

Transportation

Main article: Transportation in metropolitan Detroit

With its proximity to Canada and its facilities, ports, major highways, rail connections and international airports, Detroit is an important transportation hub. The city has three international border crossings, the Ambassador Bridge, Detroit-Windsor Tunnel and Michigan Central Railway Tunnel, linking Detroit to Windsor, Ontario. The Ambassador Bridge is the single busiest border crossing in North America, carrying 27% of the total trade between the U.S. and Canada.

Air

Detroit Metropolitan Wayne County Airport (DTW), the area's principal airport, is located in nearby Romulus and is a primary hub for Delta Air Lines and a secondary hub for Spirit Airlines. Bishop International Airport (FNT) in Flint, Michigan is the second busiest commercial airport in the region. Coleman A. Young International Airport (DET), previously called Detroit City Airport, is on Detroit's northeast side. Although Southwest Airlines once flew from the airport, the airport now maintains only charter service and general aviation. Willow Run Airport, in far-western Wayne County near Ypsilanti, is a general aviation and cargo airport.

Mass transit

People Mover train comes into the Renaissance Center station

Mass transit in the region is provided by bus services. Ridership on the region's mass transit systems increased by 8.4% in 2006. The Detroit Department of Transportation (DDOT) provides service to the outer edges of the city. From there, the Suburban Mobility Authority for Regional Transportation (SMART) provides service to the suburbs. Cross border service between the downtown areas of Windsor and Detroit is provided by Transit Windsor via the Tunnel Bus. It is also possible for those who cross to Detroit on the tunnel bus to use a Transit Windsor transfer for transfers onto Detroit Smart buses, allowing for travel around Metro Detroit from a single fare.

An elevated rail system known as the People Mover, completed in 1987, provides daily service around a 2.9 miles (4.7 km) loop downtown. The Woodward Avenue Light Rail, beginning in 2013, will serve as a link between the Detroit People Mover and SEMCOG Commuter Rail which extends from Detroit's New Center area to The Henry Ford, Dearborn, Detroit Metropolitan Airport, Ypsilanti, and Ann Arbor Amtrak provides service to Detroit, operating its *Wolverine* service between Chicago and Pontiac. Baggage cannot be checked at this location; however, up to two suitcases in addition to any "personal items" such as briefcases, purses, laptop bags, and infant equipment are allowed on board as carry-ons. The Amtrak station is located in the New Center area north of downtown. The J.W. Westcott II, which delivers mail to lake freighters on the Detroit River, is the world's only floating post office.

Freeways

Main article: Roads and freeways in metropolitan Detroit

Metro Detroit has an extensive toll-free expressway system administered by the Michigan Department of Transportation. Four major Interstate Highways surround the city. Detroit is connected via Interstate 75 and Interstate 96 to Kings Highway 401 and to major Southern Ontario cities such as London, Ontario and the Greater Toronto Area. I-75 (The Chrysler and Fisher Freeways) is the region's main north-south route, serving Flint, Pontiac, Troy, and Detroit, before continuing south (as the Detroit-Toledo and Seaway Freeways) to serve many of the communities along the shore of Lake Erie.

I-94 (The Edsel Ford Freeway) runs east-west through Detroit and serves Ann Arbor to the west (where it continues to Chicago) and Port Huron to the northeast. The stretch of the current I-94 freeway from Ypsilanti to Detroit was one of America's earlier limited-access highways. Henry Ford built it to link the factories at Willow Run and Dearborn during World War II. A portion was known as the Willow Run Expressway. I-96 runs northwest-southeast through Livingston, Oakland and Wayne Counties and (as the Jeffries Freeway through Wayne County) has its eastern terminus in downtown Detroit.

I-275 runs north-south from I-75 in the south to the junction of I-96 and I-696 in the north, providing a bypass through the western suburbs of Detroit. I-375 (The Chrysler Spur) is a short spur route in downtown Detroit, an extension of the Chrysler Freeway. I-696 (The Reuther Freeway) runs east-west from the junction of I-96 and I-275, providing a route through the northern suburbs of Detroit. Taken together, I-275 and I-696 form a semicircle around Detroit. Michigan State highways designated with the letter M serve to connect major freeways.

Surrounding municipalities

The cities of Hamtramck and Highland Park both lie entirely within the boundaries of the city of Detroit.

See also

- Cycling in Detroit
- Detroit in literature
- Northern Cities Shift
- Saginaw Trail
- Images of Detroit
- Images of Metro Detroit
- List of films set in Detroit
- List of people from Detroit
- List of songs about Detroit
- List of tallest buildings in Detroit

Further reading

- Bak, Richard (2001). *Detroit Across 3 Centuries*. Thompson Gale. ISBN 1585360015.
- Burton, Clarence M (1896). *Cadillac's Village: A History of the Settlement, 1701–1710*. Detroit Society for Genealogical Research. ISBN 0-943112-21-4.
- Burton, Clarence M (1912). *Early Detroit: A sketch of some of the interesting affairs of the olden time*. Burton Abstracts. OCLC 926958 [2].
- Catlin, George B. (1923). *The Story of Detroit* [3]. The Detroit News Association.
- Chafets, Zev (1990). *Devil's Night: And Other True Tales of Detroit*. Random House. ISBN 0-394-58525-9.
- Dunnigan, Brian Leigh (2001). *Frontier Metropolis, Picturing Early Detroit, 1701–1838*. Great Lakes Books. ISBN 0-814-32767-2.
- Farley, Reynolds, et al. (2002). *Detroit Divided*. Russell Sage Foundation Publications. ISBN 0-87154-281-1.
- Farmer, Silas (1889). *History of Detroit and Wayne County and Early Michigan*. Omnigraphics Inc; Reprint edition (October 1998). ISBN 1-55888-991-4.
- Gavrilovich, Peter and Bill McGraw (2000). *The Detroit Almanac*. Detroit Free Press. ISBN 0-937247-34-0.
- Hill, Eric J. and John Gallagher (2002). *AIA Detroit: The American Institute of Architects Guide to Detroit Architecture*. Wayne State University Press. ISBN 0-8143-3120-3.
- Meyer, Katherine Mattingly and Martin C.P. McElroy with Introduction by W. Hawkins Ferry, Hon A.I.A. (1980). *Detroit Architecture A.I.A. Guide Revised Edition*. Wayne State University Press.

ISBN 0-8143-1651-4.
- Parkman, Francis (1994). *The Conspiracy of Pontiac*. University of Nebraska Press. ISBN 0-8032-8737-2.
- Poremba, David Lee (2003). *Detroit: A Motor City History (Images of America)*. Arcadia Publishing. ISBN 0-7385-2435-2.
- Powell, L. P (1901). "Detroit, the Queen City," *Historic Towns of the Western States* (New York).
- Sharoff, Robert (2005). *American City: Detroit Architecture*. Wayne State University Press. ISBN 0-8143-3270-6.
- Sobocinski, Melanie Grunow (2005). *Detroit and Rome: building on the past*. Regents of the University of Michigan. ISBN 0933691092.
- Stahl, Kenneth (2009). *The Great Rebellion: A Socio-economic Analysis of the 1967 Detroit Riot*. ISBN 978-0-9799157-0-3.
- Sugrue, Thomas J (1998). *The Origins of the Urban Crisis*. Princeton University Press. ISBN 0-691-05888-1.
- Woodford, Arthur M. (2001). *This is Detroit 1701–2001*. Wayne State University Press. ISBN 0-8143-2914-4.

External links

- Current Conditions for Detroit, MI [4] - At weather.com [5]

Municipal government and local Chamber of Commerce

- City of Detroit official website [1]
- Detroit Metro Convention & Visitors Bureau [6]
- Detroit Regional Chamber of Commerce [7]

Visitor's Guide

- Detroit travel guide from Wikitravel

Historical research and current events

- Detroit Entertainment District [8]
- Detroit Historical Museums & Society [9]
- Detroit Riverfront Conservancy [10]
- Experience Detroit [11]
- Virtual Motor City Collection [12] at Wayne State University Library, contains over 30,000 images of Detroit from 1890 to 1980

1. REDIRECT Template:Navboxes

Metro Detroit

Metro Detroit Detroit–Warren–Livonia MSA Detroit–Ann Arbor–Flint CSA	
— CSA —	
Cranbrook Art Museum (top left) in Bloomfield Hills and The Henry Ford (top center) in Dearborn are National Historic Landmarks.	
 A simulated-color satellite image of Metro Detroit, with Windsor across the river, taken on NASA's Landsat 7 satellite.	
Country	United States
State	Michigan
Largest city	Detroit
Counties	
Area	
- **Urban**	1261.4 sq mi (3267 km^2)
- **MSA**	3913 sq mi (10134.6 km^2)
- **CSA**	5814 sq mi (15058.2 km^2)
Elevation	569–1,280 ft (173–390 m)
Population (2009 est.)	
- **Urban**	3,903,377 (9th)
- **MSA**	4,403,437 (11th)
- **CSA**	5,327,764 (11th)
	MSA/CSA = 2009, Urban = 2000

Time zone	EST (UTC-5)
- Summer (DST)	EDT (UTC-4)
Area code(s)	248, 313, 586, 734, 810, 947

The **Detroit metropolitan area**, often referred to as **Metro Detroit**, is the metropolitan area located in Southeast Michigan centered on the city of Detroit. The Detroit metropolitan area is the second largest U.S. metropolitan area linking the Great Lakes system. U.S. Army TACOM Life Cycle Management Command (TACOM) is headquartered in Metro Detroit together with Selfridge Air National Guard Base. As a major metropolitan area, it is known for its automotive heritage, arts, and popular music legacies.

Definitions

See also: Michigan census statistical areas

At its core, Metro Detroit comprises the counties of Wayne, Oakland, and Macomb. These counties are sometimes referred to informally as the **Detroit Tri-County Area** and had an estimated population of 3,962,783 as of 2009.

The **Detroit Urban Area**, which serves as the core of the Metropolitan Statistical Area, ranks as the 9th most populous of the United States, with a population of 3,903,377 as of the 2000 census, and area of 1261.4 square miles (3267 km^2).

The United States Office of Management and Budget defines the **Detroit–Warren–Livonia** Metropolitan Statistical Area (MSA) as the six counties of Lapeer, Livingston, Macomb, Oakland, St. Clair, and Wayne. As of the 2000 census, the MSA had a population of 4,441,551. The Census Bureau's 2009 estimate placed the population at 4,403,437, which ranks it as the eleventh-largest MSA. The MSA covers an area of 3913 square miles (10130 km^2).

The nine-county area designated by the United States Census Bureau as the **Detroit–Ann Arbor–Flint** Combined Statistical Area (CSA) includes the three additional counties of Genesee, Monroe, and Washtenaw, the metropolitan areas of Flint, Ann Arbor, and Monroe, plus the Detroit-Warren-Livonia MSA. It had a population of 5,357,538 as of the 2000 census. The Census Bureau's 2009 estimate placed the population at 5,327,764. This CSA covers an area of 5814 square miles (15060 km^2). Lenawee County was removed from Detroit's CSA in 2000.

With the adjacent city of Windsor, Ontario and its suburbs, the combined **Windsor-Detroit** area has a population of about 5.7 million. When the nearby Toledo Metropolitan Area and its commuters are taken into account, the region constitutes a much larger population center. An estimated 46 million people live within a 300-mile (480 km) radius of Detroit proper. Metro Detroit is at the center of the Great Lakes Megalopolis.

Economy

Main article: Economy of metropolitan Detroit

See also: List of companies based in Michigan

The region's nine county area with its population of 5.4 million has a workforce of about 2.6 million with about 247,000 businesses. Metro Detroit has made Michigan's economy a leader in information technology, biotechnology, and advanced manufacturing; Michigan ranks fourth nationally in high tech employment with 568,000 high tech workers, including 70,000 in the automotive industry. Michigan typically ranks second or third in overall Research & development (R&D) expenditures in the United States. Metro Detroit is an important source of engineering job opportunities. As the home of the "Big Three" American automakers (General Motors, Ford, and Chrysler), it is the world's traditional automotive center and a key pillar of the U.S. economy. For the first half of 2010, the domestic automakers have reported significant profits indicating the beginning of rebound.

In July 2010, the metro area unemployemnt rate was 14.1 percent, during the recession. Metro Detroit shared in the economic difficulties brought on by the severe stock market decline following the September 11, 2001 attacks which had caused a pension and benefit fund crisis for American companies including General Motors, Ford, and Chrysler. In the 2000s, the domestic auto industry accounts, directly and indirectly, for one of ten jobs in the United States making it a significant component for economic recovery.

The Renaissance Center, GM's world headquarters

During the Economic crisis of 2008, President George W. Bush extended loans from the Troubled Assets Relief Program (TARP) funds in order to help the Big three automakers bridge the recession. The President extended the loans to aid the auto industry's restructuring plans which include a goal to convert long term debt into equity and to make costs competitive.

In spite of these efforts, the severity of the recession required Detroit's automakers to take additional steps to restructure, including idling many plants. With the U.S. Treasury extending the necessary debtor in possession financing, Chrysler and GM filed separate 'pre-packaged' Chapter 11 restructurings in May and June 2009 respectively.

Metro Detroit serves as the headquarters for the United States Army TACOM Life Cycle Management Command (TACOM), with Selfridge Air National Guard Base. Detroit Metropolitan Airport (DTW) is one of America's largest and most recently modernized facilities, with six major runways, Boeing 747 maintenance facilities, and an attached Westin Hotel and Conference Center.

Detroit has major port status and an extensive toll-free expressway system. A 2004 Border Transportation Partnership study showed that 150,000 jobs in the Detroit-Windsor region and $13 billion in annual production depend on Detroit's international border crossing. A source of top talent, the University of Michigan in Ann Arbor is one of the world's leading research institutions, and Wayne State University in

Southfield Town Center

Detroit has the largest single-campus medical school in the United States.

In 2004, led by Metro Detroit, Michigan ranked second nationally in new corporate facilities and expansions. From 1997 to 2004, Michigan was the only state to top the 10,000 mark for the number of major new developments. Metro Detroit is a leading corporate location with major office complexes such as the Renaissance Center, the Southfield Town Center, and Cadillac Place with the Fisher Building in the historic New Center area. Both BorgWarner and TRW Automotive Holdings chose Metro Detroit for their new headquarters. Quicken Loans, Ernst & Young, Ally Financial, Visteon, and OnStar are sources of growth.

Compuware, IBM, Google, and Covansys are examples information technology and software companies with a headquarters or major presence in Metro Detroit. HP Enterprise Services makes Metro Detroit its regional headquarters, and one of its largest global employment locations. The metropolitan Detroit area has one of the nation's largest office markets with 147,082,003 square feet. Virtually every major U.S company and many from around the globe have a presence in Metro Detroit. Chrysler's largest corporate facility is its U.S. headquarters and technology center in the Detroit suburb of Auburn Hills. In decade leading up to 2006, downtown Detroit gained more than $15 billion in new investment from private and public sectors.

Tourism

Main articles: Architecture of metropolitan Detroit, Tourism in metropolitan Detroit, and Culture of Detroit

Tourism is an important component of the region's culture and economy, comprising nine percent of the area's two million jobs. About 15.9 million people visit metro Detroit annually, spending about $4.8 billion. Detroit is the largest city or metro area in the U.S. to offer casino resorts (MGM Grand Detroit, MotorCity Casino, Greektown Casino, and nearby Caesars Windsor).

Metro Detroit is a tourist destination easily accommodating super-sized crowds to events such as the North American International Auto Show, the Windsor-Detroit International Freedom Festival, 2009 NCAA Final Four, and Super Bowl XL. The Detroit International Riverfront links the Renaissance Center a series of venues, parks, restaurants, and hotels. In 2006, the four-day Motown Winter Blast drew a cold weather crowd of about 1.2 million people to Campus Martius Park area downtown.

Detroit's metroparks include fresh water beaches such as Metropolitan Beach, Kensington Beach, and Stony Creek Beach. Metro Detroit offers canoeing through the Huron-Clinton Metroparks as well as downhill and cross-county skiing at Alpine Valley Ski Resort, Mt. Brighton, Mt. Holly, and Pine Knob Ski Resort. The Detroit River International Wildlife Refuge is the only international wildlife preserve in North America, uniquely located in the heart of a major metropolitan area. The Refuge includes islands, coastal wetlands, marshes, shoals, and waterfront lands along 48 miles (77 km) of the Detroit River and Western Lake Erie shoreline.

Metro Detroit contains a number of shopping malls, including the upscale Somerset Collection in Troy and the Great Lakes Crossing outlet mall in Auburn Hills, both major draws for tourists.

Detroit Institute of Arts.

The region's leading attraction is The Henry Ford, located in the Detroit suburb of Dearborn, which is America's largest indoor-outdoor museum complex. The recent renovation of the Renaissance Center, a state of the art cruise ship dock, new stadiums, and a new RiverWalk have spurred economic development. Nearby Windsor has a 19 year old drinking age with a myriad of entertainment to complement Detroit's Greektown district. Tourism planners have yet to tap the potential economic impact of the estimated 46 million people that live within a 300-mile (480-km) radius of Detroit.

Demographics

See also: Michigan locations by per capita income

The first Europeans to colonize the Detroit area were French, and their legacy can be observed today in the names of many area cities (ex. Detroit, Grosse Pointe, Grosse Ile) and streets (ex. Gratiot, Beaubien, St. Antoine, Cadieux). Later, there was an influx of persons of British and German descent, followed later by Polish, Irish, Italian, Lebanese, Assyrian/Chaldean, Greek, Jewish, and Belgian immigrants who made their way to the area in the early 20 century and during and after World War II. There was a large migration into the city of from the rural South following World War I.

Today, the Detroit suburbs in Oakland County, Macomb County, and northeastern and northwestern Wayne County are predominantly white. Oakland County is among the most affluent counties in the United States with populations over one million. In Wayne County, the city of Dearborn has a large concentration of Arab Americans, mainly Lebanese. Recently, the area has witnessed some growth in Albanian American, Asian American and Hispanic populations. Immigration continues to play a role in the region's projected growth with the population of Detroit-Ann Arbor-Flint (CMSA) estimated to be 6,191,000 by 2025.

In the 2000s, 70% of the total Black population in Metro Detroit lived in the City of Detroit. Of the 185 cities and townships in Metro Detroit, 115 were over 95% White. Of the more than 240,000 suburban blacks in Metro Detroit, 44% lived in Inkster, Oak Park, Pontiac, and Southfield; 9/10ths of the African-American population in the area consisted of residents of Detroit, Highland Park, Inkster, Pontiac, and Southfield.

	Metro Detroit
Central City	Detroit[†] (Hamtramck, Highland Park)
Suburbs over 80,000	Canton Township • Clinton Township • Dearborn • Farmington Hills • Livonia • Sterling Heights • Troy • Warren • Westland
Suburbs 50,000 - 80,000	Dearborn Heights • Farmington Hills • Grosse Pointe • Macomb Township • Novi • Pontiac • Redford Township • Rochester Hills • Royal Oak • Saint Clair Shores • Shelby Township • Southfield • Taylor • Waterford Township • West Bloomfield Township
Satellite cities	Adrian • Ann Arbor • Brighton • Flint • Howell • Jackson • Lapeer • Monroe • Port Huron • Windsor

Counties in MSA	Lapeer • Livingston • Macomb • Oakland • St. Clair • Wayne
Counties in CSA	Genesee • Monroe • Washtenaw
Region	Southeast Michigan • Great Lakes
Outlying regions	Central Michigan • Flint/Tri-Cities • Northwest Ohio • Southwestern Ontario
Topics	Architecture · Culture · Detroit River · Economy · Freeways · History · Historic places · International Riverfront · Lake St. Clair · Media · Music · Parks and beaches · People · Skyscrapers · Sports · Theatre · Tourism · Transportation
† - Wayne County Seat.	

Transportation

Main article: Transportation in metropolitan Detroit

Major airports

- Ann Arbor Municipal Airport (ARB)
- Coleman A. Young International Airport (DET) (Detroit) - General aviation only
- Detroit Metropolitan Wayne County Airport (DTW) (Romulus) - Major commercial airport, hub for Delta Airlines and Spirit Airlines
- Flint-Bishop International Airport(FNT) (Flint) - Commercial airport
- Oakland County International Airport (PTK) Waterford Township) - Charter passenger facility

Detroit Metropolitan Airport is the region's major international airport. The McNamara Terminal's ExpressTram is used to transport passengers from one end of the terminal to the other

- St. Clair County International Airport (near Port Huron, Michigan) - An international airport on the U.S. and Canadian Border.
- Selfridge Air National Guard Base (Mount Clemens) - Military airbase
- Willow Run Airport (YIP) (Ypsilanti) - Cargo, general aviation, charter passenger traffic

Transit systems

Bus service for the metropolitan area is provided jointly by the Detroit Department of Transportation (DDOT) and Suburban Mobility Authority for Regional Transportation (SMART) which operate under a cooperative service and fare agreement. The Woodward Avenue Light Rail, beginning in 2013, will serve as a link between the Detroit People Mover monorail which encircles the downtown and SEMCOG Commuter Rail which extends from Detroit's New Center area to The Henry Ford, Dearborn, Detroit Metropolitan Airport, Ypsilanti, and Ann Arbor

Roads and freeways

Main article: Roads and freeways in metropolitan Detroit

The Metro Detroit area is linked by a advanced network of major roads and freeways which include Interstate highways. Traditionally, Detroiters refer to some of their freeways by name rather than route number. The Davison, Lodge, and Southfield freeways are almost always referred to by name rather than route number. Detroiters commonly precede freeway names with the word 'the' as in the Lodge, the Southfield, and the Davison. Those without names are referred to by number.

Surface street navigation in Metro Detroit is commonly anchored by "mile roads", major east-west surface streets that are spaced at one-mile intervals and increment as one travels north and away from the city center. Mile roads sometimes have two names, the numeric name (ex. 15 Mile Road) used in Macomb County and a local name (ex. Maple Road) used in Oakland County mostly.

Education

See also: List of high schools in Michigan

University of Michigan.

- Ave Maria College, Ypsilanti
- Cleary University, Ann Arbor and Howell
- College for Creative Studies, Detroit
- Concordia University, Ann Arbor
- Cranbrook Academy of Art, Bloomfield Hills
- Davenport University
- Dorsey Business School
- Eastern Michigan University, Ypsilanti
- Henry Ford Community College, Dearborn
- Kettering University, Flint
- Lawrence Technological University, Southfield
- Macomb Community College, Warren and Clinton Township
- Madonna University, Livonia
- Marygrove College, Detroit
- Michigan State University, Troy
- Monroe County Community College, Monroe
- Mott Community College, Flint
- Northwood University
- Oakland Community College
- Oakland University, Rochester
- Rochester College, Rochester Hills
- Schoolcraft College, Livonia
- Specs Howard School of Media Arts, Southfield
- Sacred Heart Major Seminary, Detroit
- SS. Cyril and Methodius Seminary, Orchard Lake
- University of Detroit Mercy, Detroit
- University of Michigan, Ann Arbor
- University of Michigan–Dearborn
- University of Michigan-Flint
- Thomas M. Cooley Law School, Auburn Hills
- Walsh College of Accountancy and Business, Troy
- Washtenaw Community College, Ann Arbor
- Wayne County Community College,
- Wayne State University, Detroit

Area codes

Metro Detroit is served by eight telephone area codes (ten if Windsor is included). The 313 area code, which used to encompass all of Southeast Michigan, has been narrowed to the city of Detroit and a few close suburbs.

- The 248 area code along with the newer 947 area code overlay mostly serve Oakland County.
- Macomb County is largely served by 586.
- Genesee, St. Clair, and Lapeer counties, as well as eastern Livingston County are covered by 810.
- Washtenaw, Monroe, and western Wayne are in the 734 area.
- The Windsor area (and most of southwestern Ontario) is served by 519 and 226.

Sports

See also: Sports in metropolitan Detroit

Professional sports has a major fan following in Metro Detroit. The area is home to many sports teams, including six professional teams in four major sports. The area's several universities field teams in a variety of sports. Michigan Stadium, home of the Michigan Wolverines, is the largest American football stadium in the world. Metro Detroit hosts many annual sporting events including auto and hydroplane racing. The area has hosted many major sporting events, including the 1994 FIFA World Cup, Super Bowl XVI, Super Bowl XL, the 2005 Major League Baseball All-Star Game, and the first two games of the 2006 World Series.

Club	Sport	League	Venue	Location
Detroit Lions	Football	NFL (National Football Conference)	Ford Field	Detroit
Detroit Red Wings	Ice hockey	NHL (Western Conference)	Joe Louis Arena	Detroit
Detroit Pistons	Basketball	NBA (Eastern Conference)	Palace of Auburn Hills	Auburn Hills
Detroit Tigers	Baseball	MLB (American League)	Comerica Park	Detroit
Eastern Michigan University	various	NCAA (Mid-American Conference)	various including Rynearson Stadium and The EMU Convocation Center	Ypsilanti
Oakland University Golden Grizzlies	various	NCAA (The Summit League)	various	Rochester
University of Detroit Mercy Titans	various	NCAA (Horizon League)	various, including Calihan Hall	Detroit
University of Michigan Wolverines	various	NCAA (Big Ten Conference, Central Collegiate Hockey Association)	various, including Michigan Stadium	Ann Arbor
Wayne State University Warriors	various	NCAA (Great Lakes Intercollegiate Athletic Conference, College Hockey America)	various	Detroit
various	Auto racing	NASCAR, IRL, ARCA	Michigan International Speedway	Brooklyn
Detroit APBA Gold Cup	Hydroplane racing	APBA	Detroit River	Detroit
Detroit Ignition	Indoor soccer	Xtreme Soccer League	Compuware Arena	Plymouth Township
Plymouth Whalers	Hockey	Ontario Hockey League	Compuware Arena	Plymouth Township
Detroit Waza	indoor soccer	PASL	Compuware Arena	Plymouth Township

See also

- Detroit travel guide from Wikitravel
- Images of Metro Detroit

External links

- Clarke Historical Library, Central Michigan University, Bibliography on Michigan (arranged by counties and regions) [6]
- Michigan Geology -- Clarke Historical Library, Central Michigan University. [1]
- List of Museums, other attractions compiled by state government. [2]
- Michigan's Official Economic Development and Travel Site. [3]
- USCG's complete list of Michigan lighthouses. [4]
- Map of Michigan Lighthouse [5] in PDF Format.
- Glorious Detroit [6]

Things to Do and See in Troy

Somerset Collection

The Grand Court at Somerset North incorporates a full glass dome.	
Location	2800 W. Big Beaver Troy, Michigan ▆▆ United States
Opening date	1969 (Somerset Mall) 1992 (Somerset South) 1996 (Somerset North)
Developer	Forbes/Cohen
Management	The Forbes Company
Owner	The Forbes Company & Frankel Associates
Architect	JPRA Architects Peterhansrea Designs
No. of stores and services	180
No. of anchor tenants	4
Total retail floor area	1450000 sq ft (134700 m^2)
Parking	7,000 spaces Surface parking, covered parking, and valet.
No. of floors	2 (Somerset South) 3 (Somerset North)
Website	The Somerset Collection [1]

Somerset Collection is an upscale shopping mall with over 180 stores located in the Metro Detroit suburb and commercial area of Troy, Michigan. Developed, managed and co-owned by The Forbes Company, the center is anchored by department stores Nordstrom, Macy's, Neiman Marcus, and Saks Fifth Avenue.

More than 180 additional specialty shops and restaurants are located at Somerset, including Tiffany & Co., Louis Vuitton, Barneys Co-op, Crate and Barrel, P.F. Chang's China Bistro, J. Alexander's, Brio Tuscan Grille, McCormick & Schmick's, The Capital Grille, California Pizza Kitchen, and the Peacock Café food court.

Somerset Collection is among the most profitable malls in the United States not owned by a real estate investment trust. Mall developers consider Somerset Collection to be among the nation's top privately held mall properties with 2004 annual sales of about $600 million and sales per square foot at $620 compared to the national average of $341, well above the "Class A" threshold. Of the 100 most profitable malls, 76 are owned by real estate investment trusts.

History

In 1967, Saks Fifth Avenue opened a stand-alone store on Big Beaver Road in the Detroit suburb of Troy. In 1969, a one floor upscale "Somerset Mall" designed by Louis G. Redstone Associates would be built onto the existing Saks, anchored by it and a new Bonwit Teller. Bonwit significantly renovated its store in 1988, only to close in 1990 after the chain went bankrupt. In 1991-1992 the center was renamed Somerset Collection, a second level was added, and Neiman Marcus opened a store on the site of the razed Bonwit Teller. Completed in August 1992, Tiffany's joined at this time as well.

Following the success of the revamped mall, co-owners Forbes/Cohen Properties and Frankel Associates opened an all new three-story $200 million 940000 sq ft (87300 m^2) expansion across Big Beaver Road in 1996, designed by JPRA Architects. Michigan's first Nordstrom and a Hudson's (now Macy's) anchored the new three-story expansion, named Somerset North. Joining the two malls is a 700-foot (210 m) enclosed bridge with a moving "Skywalk" over Big Beaver Road. Somerset North contains the Collection's food court, and both North and South feature upscale, independent restaurants. Somerset North's Grand Court features a full arched glass dome roof. JPRA incorporated a similar large arched glass ceiling into its design for The Mall at Millenia, another upscale mall in Orlando, Florida also owned by The Forbes Company.

The expanded Somerset Collection contains 1450000 sq ft (134700 m^2) of gross leasable area anchored by a 300000 sq ft (27900 m^2) Macy's, a 240000 sq ft (22300 m^2) Nordstrom, a 160000 sq ft (14900 m^2) Saks Fifth Avenue, and a 141000 sq ft (13100 m^2) Neiman-Marcus.

Restaurants

The third level of the Somerset Collection North features a grouping of ten eateries which are called The Peacock Cafes, with combined seating for 650 patrons. Somerset Collection North includes restaurants such as The Capital Grille, J.Alexander's, and California Pizza Kitchen. The Bistro at Macy's and Nordstrom Cafe are also available. Somerset Collection South includes P. F. Chang's China Bistro, Brio Tuscan Grille, McCormick & Schmick's, and the Neiman Marcus Cafe.

Features

Both Somerset Collection North and Somerset Collection South feature distinctive design elements and architectural features. An exterior of Cranbrook brick and Mankato stone is combined with interior finishes of marble, woods, a continuous skylight, fountains, stages for the performing arts and a number of original sculptures. Spanning Big Beaver Road and integrating the twin centers is a 700-foot (210 m), enclosed, climate-controlled Skywalk. One of the first skywalks of its kind in the country, the bridge features a moving sidewalk to move shoppers between Somerset Collection South

One of the two Granite Sorvikivi Floating Stone spheres at Somerset Collection North.

and Somerset Collection North. Somerset Collection features over 180 shops and restaurants. Of the mall's 180 stores, 78 are unique to this center as the only Michigan location. Stores include Louis Vuitton, Gucci, Ralph Lauren, Neiman Marcus, Saks Fifth Avenue, Tiffany & Co., and Crate & Barrel. The mall offers valet parking where the car may be delivered to the Somerset North or South entrance. The mall has a full service concierge staff.

Sorvikivi Floating Stone Fountain

The Sorvikivi Floating Stone fountains are both found at Somerset Collection North in the Grand Court. They were made in Finland and are made out of Amadeus granite, which is a combination of charcoal gray with magenta streaks. The ball weighs more than 2 tons and is 40 inches in diameter. Because of the large surface area, the ball requires very little water pressure to keep it aloft. The amount of pressure required is surprisingly small to keep it aloft; around 10 to 15 pounds per square inch. The water falls into a black granite trough, which sits within a raised base of Mankato stone, a chop-top pyramid five feet high.

Special events

Special events are hosted at Somerset Collection by not only the mall but individual stores. These events include yoga classes, special savings, visiting Santa, fashion shows, and other events.

Guest services

The concierge service at Somerset Collection includes a variety of services including gift wrapping, stroller and wheelchair rental, Wi-Fi internet access at the Somerset North Grand Court, Peacock Cafe's, and Somerset South Rotundra. Valet parking is available.

Statistics

Building	Image	Levels	Area sq ft / m²
Somerset North		3	940,000 / 87,300
Macy's		3	300,000 / 27,900
Nordstrom		3	240,000 / 22,300
Somerset South		2	500,000 / 46,500
Neiman Marcus		2	141,000 / 13,100
Saks Fifth Avenue		2	160,000 / 14,900
Moving skywalk		2	700 ft. (213 m.) Access level 2.
Gross leasable area		2-3	1,450,000 / 134,700

Gallery

See also

- Architecture of metropolitan Detroit
- Economy of metropolitan Detroit
- Metro Detroit
- Tourism in metropolitan Detroit

References and further reading

- Cantor, George (2005). *Detroit: An Insiders Guide to Michigan.* University of Michigan Press. ISBN 0472030922.
- Garvin, Alexander (2002). *The American City: What Works What Doesn't (2nd Ed.).* McGraw Hill. ISBN 9780071373678.
- Meyer, Katherine Mattingly and Martin C.P. McElroy with Introduction by W. Hawkins Ferry, Hon A.I.A. (1980). *Detroit Architecture A.I.A. Guide Revised Edition.* Wayne State University Press. ISBN 0-8143-1651-4.
- Urban Land Institute (1994). *ULI Market Profiles.* Urban Land Institute.

External links

- Somerset Collection website [1]
- The Forbes Company website [2]

Geographical coordinates: 42°33′41″N 83°11′2″W

Oakland Mall

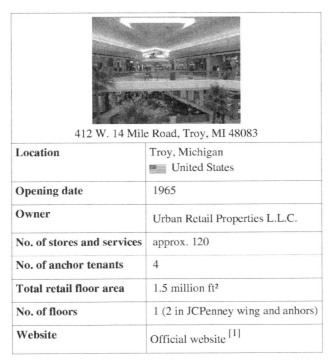

412 W. 14 Mile Road, Troy, MI 48083	
Location	Troy, Michigan ▰▰ United States
Opening date	1965
Owner	Urban Retail Properties L.L.C.
No. of stores and services	approx. 120
No. of anchor tenants	4
Total retail floor area	1.5 million ft²
No. of floors	1 (2 in JCPenney wing and anhors)
Website	Official website [1]

Oakland Mall is an enclosed shopping mall located in the city of Troy, Michigan which is a suburb of Detroit, Michigan. It is located in the northwest corner of 14 Mile Rd. & John R. Rd. intersection, adjacent to I-75 (Chrysler Freeway). The mall features about 120 stores, including a food court, plus several big box stores on the periphery. The mall has 1500000 square feet (140000 m²).

History

The first store to open at the site of the Oakland Mall was Sears, which opened in 1965. In 1968, the mall itself opened, featuring Hudson's, Wrigley Supermarket, and Kresge. Wrigley Supermarket was later converted to J. C. Penney in the late 1970s. This store was torn down for a northern expansion, which opened in 1980. This new wing, unlike the original mall, was two stories, featuring a new J. C. Penney store and a movie theater.

The older one level mall.

In 1987, S. S. Kresge closed and was replaced with smaller stores. A food court was added to the mall in the late 1990s, replacing a former combination Burger King/Godfather's Pizza. Borders opened in the late 1990s. The movie theaters were closed in 2000 and were later converted to Steve & Barry's, which itself closed in early 2009. Hudson's was converted to Marshall Field's in 2001. In 2004, Lord & Taylor was proposed to become the mall's fourth department store; however, the store never materialized. September 2006 saw the conversion of Marshall Field's (and other May Co. nameplates) to the Macy's name. In late 2009, Famous Labels opened its first Michigan store in the previous Steve & Barry's location.

External links

- Official website [1]
- Aerial Photo from Google Maps [2]

Top of Troy

Top of Troy	
General information	
Location	Troy, Michigan United States
Status	Complete
Constructed	1975 International style
Use	Office/retail
Height	
Top floor	346 ft (106 m)
Technical details	
Floor count	25
Companies involved	
Architect(s)	Rossetti

The **Top of Troy** stands at 755 West Big Beaver Road, in Troy, Michigan. It is the tallest building in Troy, Michigan. PNC Financial Services maintains regional offices in the building as the major tenant. The triangular-shaped high-rise was constructed in 1974, and completed in 1975. It stands 25 stories (346 ft/106m), and is used mainly for office space, retail, and restaurant uses. It was designed in the international style of architecture. Its main materials are concrete and glass.

The building can be easily accessed from Interstate 75, as it is located just west of the interchange (I-75 exit number 69) with Big Beaver Road. The Top of Troy can be seen for miles from much of the Metro Detroit area.

Description

- Architect: Rossetti architects
- This triangle-shaped tower has been the tallest building in Troy since its completion.

See also

- Architecture of metropolitan Detroit
- Metro Detroit
- Tourism in metropolitan Detroit

References

- Fisher, Dale (2005). *Southeast Michigan: Horizons of Growth*. Grass Lake, MI: Eyry of the Eagle Publishing. ISBN 1891143255.
- Meyer, Katherine Mattingly and Martin C.P. McElroy with Introduction by W. Hawkins Ferry, Hon A.I.A. (1980). *Detroit Architecture A.I.A. Guide Revised Edition*. Wayne State University Press. ISBN 0-8143-1651-4.

External links

- Official Website [1]
- Google Maps location of Top of Troy [2]
- Top of Troy Building at Emporis.com [3]
- SkyscraperPage.com's Profile on Top of Troy [4]

Geographical coordinates: 42°33′37″N 83°9′39″W

Attractions

Detroit Red Wings

Detroit Red Wings	
2010–11 Detroit Red Wings season	
Conference	Western
Division	Central
Founded	1926
History	**Detroit Cougars** 1926–30 **Detroit Falcons** 1930–32 **Detroit Red Wings** 1932–present
Home arena	Joe Louis Arena
City	Detroit, Michigan
Colors	Red, white
Media	Fox Sports Detroit WXYT (1270 AM, 97.1 FM)
Owner(s)	Mike Ilitch
General manager	Ken Holland
Head coach	Mike Babcock
Captain	Nicklas Lidstrom
Minor league affiliates	Grand Rapids Griffins (AHL) Toledo Walleye (ECHL)
Stanley Cups	**11** (1935–36, 1936–37, 1942–43, 1949–50, 1951–52, 1953–54, 1954–55, 1996–97, 1997–98, 2001–02, 2007–08)
Conference championships	**6** (1994–95, 1996–97, 1997–98, 2001–02, 2007–08, 2008–09)

Division championships	**18** (1933–34, 1935–36, 1936–37, 1987–88, 1988–89, 1991–92, 1993–94, 1994–95, 1995–96, 1998–99, 2000–01, 2001–02, 2002–03, 2003–04, 2005–06, 2006–07, 2007–08, 2008–09)

The **Detroit Red Wings** are a professional ice hockey team based in Detroit, Michigan. They are members of the Central Division of the Western Conference of the National Hockey League (NHL), and are one of the Original Six teams of the NHL.

As of 2010, the Red Wings have won the most Stanley Cup championships (11) of any NHL franchise based in the United States, and are third overall in total NHL championships, behind the Montreal Canadiens (24) and Toronto Maple Leafs (13). They currently play home games in the 20,066 capacity Joe Louis Arena after having spent over 40 years playing in Olympia Stadium.

Between the 1933–34 and 1965–66 seasons, the Red Wings missed the playoffs only four times. More recently, the Red Wings have made the playoffs in 25 of the last 27 seasons, including the last 19 in a row. This is the longest current streak of post-season appearances in all of North American professional sports.

Franchise history

For more information, see History of the Detroit Red Wings.

1926–49: Early years

Following the 1926 Stanley Cup playoffs, during which the Western Hockey League was widely reported to be on the verge of folding, the NHL held a meeting on April 17 to consider applications for expansion franchises, at which it was reported that five different groups sought a team for Detroit. During a subsequent meeting on May 15, the league approved a franchise to the Townsend-Seyburn group of Detroit and named Charles A. Hughes as governor. Frank and Lester Patrick, the owners of the WHL, made a deal to sell the league's players to the NHL and cease league operations. The new Detroit franchise purchased the players of the folded Victoria Cougars WHL club to play for the team. The new Detroit franchise also adopted the Cougars nickname in honor of the folded franchise.

Since no arena in Detroit was ready at the time, the Cougars played their first season in Windsor, Ontario at the Border Cities Arena. For the 1927–28 season, the Cougars moved into the new Detroit Olympia, which would be their home rink until December 15, 1979. This was also the first season behind the bench for Jack Adams, who would be a part of the franchise for the next 36 years as either coach or general manager.

The Cougars made the Stanley Cup playoffs for the first time in 1929 with Carson Cooper leading the team in scoring. The Cougars were outscored 7–2 in the two-game series with the Toronto Maple Leafs. In 1930, the Cougars were renamed the **Falcons**, but their woes continued, as they usually finished near the bottom of the standings, even though they made the playoffs again in 1932.

In 1932, the NHL let grain merchant James E. Norris buy the Falcons. Norris had made two previous unsuccessful bids to buy an NHL team. Norris' first act was to choose a new name — the Red Wings. Earlier in the century, Norris had played on one of hockey's early powers, the Montreal HC, nicknamed the "Winged Wheelers." Norris transformed the club's logo into the first version of the Red Wings logo as it is known today.

Norris also placed coach Jack Adams on a one-year probation for the 1932–33 NHL season. Jack Adams managed to pass his probationary period by leading the renamed franchise to winning its first ever playoff series by defeating the Montreal Maroons. Despite the success, the team lost in the semi-finals to the New York Rangers.

In 1934 the Wings made the Stanley Cup Finals for the first time, with John Sorrell scoring 21 goals over 47 games and Larry Aurie leading the team in scoring. However, the Chicago Black Hawks eliminated Detroit in the finals, winning the best-of-five series in four games and winning their own first title.

The Red Wings won their first Stanley Cup in 1936, defeating Toronto in four games. Detroit repeated its championship season in 1937, winning over the Rangers in the full five games.

In 1938, the Wings and the Montreal Canadiens were the first NHL teams to play in Europe, playing in Paris, France and London, England. The Wings played nine games against the Canadiens and went 3-5-1. The Wings did not play in Europe again until the preseason and start of the 2009-10 NHL season in Sweden against the St. Louis Blues.

They made the Stanley Cup Finals in three consecutive years during the early 1940s. In 1941 they were swept by the Boston Bruins, in 1942 they lost a seven-game series against Toronto in the finals after winning the first three games, but in 1943, with Syd Howe and Mud Bruneteau scoring 20 goals apiece, Detroit won their third Cup by sweeping the Bruins. Through the rest of the decade, the team made the playoffs every year, and reached the finals three more times.

In 1946, one of the greatest players in hockey history came into the NHL with the Red Wings. Gordie Howe, a right-winger from Floral, Saskatchewan, only scored seven goals and 15 assists in his first season and would not reach his prime for a few more years. It was also the last season as head coach for Adams, who stepped down after the season to concentrate on his duties as general manager. He was succeeded by minor league coach Tommy Ivan.

By his second season, Howe was paired with Sid Abel and Ted Lindsay to form what would become one of the great lines in NHL history—the "Production Line". Lindsay's 33 goals propelled the Wings to the Stanley Cup Finals, where they were swept by the Maple Leafs. Detroit reached the Finals again the following season, only to be swept again by Toronto.

1950–66: The Gordie Howe era

The Wings won the Stanley Cup again in 1950, with Pete Babando scoring the game winner in double overtime of game 7 to beat the Rangers in the Finals. After the game, Lindsay skated around the Olympia ice with the Cup, beginning a tradition that continues today.

After being upset by the Montreal Canadiens in the 1951 semifinals, Detroit won its fifth Cup in 1952, sweeping both the Leafs and the Canadiens, with the Production Line of Howe, Abel and Lindsay joined by second-year goalie Terry Sawchuk. Detroit would become the first team in 17 years to go undefeated in the playoffs. They also scored an amazing 24 playoff goals, compared to Toronto and Montreal's combined total of 5. Abel left the Wings for Chicago following the season, and his spot on the roster was replaced by Alex Delvecchio.

James E. Norris died in December 1952. He was succeeded as team president by his daughter, Marguerite—the first (and as of the 2006–07 season, only) woman to head an NHL franchise. She made no secret of her dislike for Adams. While she could have summarily fired him, since he was still without a contract, she chose not to do so.

Following another playoff upset in 1953 at the hands of the Bruins, the Red Wings won back to back Stanley Cups in 1954; over Montreal, when Habs defenseman Doug Harvey redirected a Tony Leswick shot into his own net; and 1955 (also over Montreal in the full seven games). The 1954–55 season ended a run of eight straight regular season titles, an NHL record.

Also during the 1955 off-season, Marguerite Norris lost an intrafamily power struggle, and was forced to turn over the Wings to younger brother Bruce, who had inherited his father's grain business. Detroit and Montreal once again met in the 1956 finals, but this time the Canadiens won the Cup, their first of five in a row.

In 1957 Ted Lindsay, who scored 30 goals and led the league in assists with 55, teamed up with Harvey to help start the NHL Players' Association and, along with outspoken young netminder Glenn Hall, was promptly traded to Chicago (which was owned by James D. Norris, Bruce's elder brother) after his most productive year.

This was one of several questionable trades made by Adams in the late 1950s. For example, a year earlier, he had traded Sawchuk to Boston; while he managed to get Sawchuk back two years later, he had to trade up-and-coming John Bucyk to do it. It was one of the most one-sided trades in hockey history; Bucyk went on to play 21 more years with the Bruins. The Wings lost in the first round of the playoffs to the Bruins. In 1959 the Red Wings missed the playoffs for the first time in 21 years.

Within a couple of years, Detroit was rejuvenated and made the Finals for four of the next six years between 1961 and 1966. However, despite having Delvecchio, Norm Ullman, Howe and Parker MacDonald as consistent goal-scorers, Lindsay's sudden one-year comeback in 1964–65, and Sawchuk and later Roger Crozier between the pipes, the Wings came away empty-handed. Adams was fired as general manager in 1963. He had coached for 15 years and served as general manager for 31 years on a handshake, and his 36–year tenure as general manager is still the longest for any general manager in NHL history.

1967–82: The "Dead Wings" era

Only a year after making the Finals, the Red Wings finished a distant fifth, 24 points out of the playoffs. It was the beginning of a slump from which they would not emerge for almost 20 years. Between 1967 and 1983, Detroit only made the playoffs twice, winning one series. From 1968 to 1982, the Wings had 14 head coaches (not counting interim coaches), with none lasting more than three seasons. In contrast, their first six full-time coaches – Art Duncan, Adams, Ivan, Jimmy Skinner and Abel – covered a 42–year period. During this dark era in franchise history, the team was derisively known as the "Dead Wings" or "Dead Things".

One factor in the Red Wings' decline was the end of the old "development" system, which allowed Adams to get young prospects to commit to playing for Detroit as early as their 16th birthday. Another factor was Ned Harkness, who was hired as coach in 1970 and was promoted to general manager midway through the season. A successful college hockey coach, Harkness tried to force his two-way style of play on a veteran Red Wings team resistant to change. The Wings chafed under his rule in which he demanded short hair, no smoking, and put other rules in place regarding drinking and phone calls. Harkness was forced to resign in 1973.

In the "expansion season" of 1967–68, the Red Wings also acquired longtime star left-winger Frank Mahovlich from the defending Cup champs in Toronto. Mahovlich would go on a line with Howe and Delvecchio, and in 1968–69, he scored a career-high 49 goals and had two All-Star seasons in Detroit.

But this could not last. Mahovlich was traded to Montreal in 1970, and Howe retired after the 1970–71 season. Howe returned to pro hockey shortly after to play with his two sons Mark and Marty Howe (Mark would later join the Red Wings at the end of his career) in the upstart World Hockey Association in 1972. Through the decade, with Mickey Redmond having two 50–goal seasons and Marcel Dionne starting to reach his prime (which he did not attain until he was traded to the Los Angeles Kings), a lack of defensive and goaltending ability continually hampered the Wings.

During 1979–80, the Wings left the Olympia for Joe Louis Arena. In 1982, after 50 years of family ownership, Bruce Norris sold the Red Wings to Mike Ilitch, founder of Little Caesars Pizza.

1983–1993: The early Yzerman era

In 1983 the Wings drafted Steve Yzerman, a center from Canada. He led the team in scoring in his rookie year, and started the Wings' climb back to the top. That season, with John Ogrodnick scoring 42 times and Ivan Boldirev and Ron Duguay also with 30–goal seasons, Detroit made the playoffs

Interior of the Joe Louis Arena, where the Red Wings have played at home since 1979, when they left the Detroit Olympia.

for the first time in six years. Defenseman Brad Park, acquired from the Boston Bruins in the 1983 free-agent market, also helped the Wings reach the postseason and ended up winning the Bill Masterton Memorial Trophy the same season.

Later Park was asked to coach the Wings, but was sacked after 45 games in 1985–86. He admitted, "I took over a last-place team, and I kept them there." They did indeed end up in the basement with a 17–57–6 record for only 40 points. This was the same year that the Wings added enforcer Bob Probert, one of the most familiar faces of the Wings in the 1980s and 1990s.

By 1987, with Yzerman, now the captain following the departure of Danny Gare, joined by Petr Klima, Adam Oates, Gerard Gallant, defenseman Darren Veitch and new head coach Jacques Demers, the Wings won a playoff series for only the second time in the modern era. They made it all the way to the conference finals against the powerful and eventual Stanley Cup champion Edmonton Oilers, but lost in five games. In 1988 they won their first division title in 23 years (since 1964–65, when they finished first in a one-division league). They did so, however, in a relatively weak division; no other team in the Norris finished above .500. As was the case in the previous season, they made it to the conference finals only to lose again to the eventual cup champion Oilers in five games.

In 1989, Yzerman scored a career-best 65 goals, but Detroit was upset in the first round by the Chicago Blackhawks. The following season Yzerman scored 62 goals, but the team missed the playoffs (the Red Wings would not miss the playoffs again under Yzerman's captaincy). Rumors spread that maybe "Stevie Wonder" should be traded.

But it was Demers, not Yzerman, who got the pink slip. New coach Bryan Murray was unable to get them back over .500, but they returned to the playoffs. Yzerman was joined by Sergei Fedorov, who would be an award-winner and frequent all-star for the team in the 1990s. In 1992, the team acquired Ray Sheppard, who had a career-best 52 goals two years later; and in '93, top defenseman Paul Coffey. Also joining the Red Wings around this time were draft picks like Slava Kozlov, Darren McCarty, Vladimir Konstantinov, and Nicklas Lidstrom.

1994–1997: The Russian Five

Former Montreal Canadiens coach Scotty Bowman got behind the Motown bench in 1993. In his second season, the lockout-shortened 1994–95 NHL season, he guided Detroit to its first Finals appearance in 29 years, only to be swept by the New Jersey Devils.

The Wings kept adding more star power, picking up Slava Fetisov, Igor Larionov, and goaltender Mike Vernon in trades and winning an NHL record 62 games in 1996. After defeating the St. Louis Blues in seven games the Wings would fall in the Western Conference Finals to the eventual champion Colorado Avalanche.

The following year, Detroit, joined by Brendan Shanahan and Larry Murphy during the season, once again reached the Finals in 1997. After defeating the St. Louis Blues, the Mighty Ducks of Anaheim and the Colorado Avalanche in the first three rounds, the Wings went on to beat the Philadelphia Flyers in four straight games in the Stanley Cup Finals. It was the Wings' first Stanley Cup since 1955, breaking the longest drought (42 years long) in the league at that time. Mike Vernon accepted the Conn Smythe Trophy as the Most Valuable Player in the 1997 playoffs.

Misfortune befell the Wings six days after their championship; defenseman Vladimir Konstantinov, one of the Wings' "Russian Five", suffered a brain injury in a limousine accident, and his career came to an abrupt end. The Red Wings dedicated the 1997–98 season, which also ended in a Stanley Cup victory, to Konstantinov, who came out onto the ice in his wheelchair on victory night to touch the Cup. The Wings won the Cup finals in another sweep, this time over the Washington Capitals. Despite his Conn Smythe Trophy in the 1997 playoffs, Mike Vernon had been replaced as the regular Wings goaltender during the season with the younger Chris Osgood. It was Osgood who minded the nets for all four games in the 1998 finals, while Steve Yzerman won the Conn Smythe.

The following season, the Wings looked poised to "three-peat" for the first time in franchise history, acquiring three-time top blueliner Chris Chelios from his hometown Chicago Blackhawks in March 1999, but they would end up losing the Western Conference Semifinals to Colorado in six games.

The Wings had built up a fierce rivalry with the Avalanche. With Colorado beating Detroit in the third round in 1996, in the second round of both 1999 and 2000, and the Red Wings beating the Avs in the third round in 1997, the battles between these two teams had become one of the fiercest in sports. During a notorious game on March 26, 1997, a brawl ensued between Colorado goalie Patrick Roy and his Detroit counterpart Mike Vernon.

In 2001, Detroit, the league's second-best team in the regular season, were upset in the playoffs by the Los Angeles Kings. During the summer that followed, they acquired goalie Dominik Hasek (the defending Vezina Trophy winner) and forwards Luc Robitaille, Brett Hull and Pavel Datsyuk. The Wings posted the league's best record in the 2001-02 regular season and defeated Colorado in seven games in the Western Conference Finals after beating the Vancouver Canucks and St. Louis Blues in rounds one and two. The Red Wings went on to capture another Stanley Cup in five games over the

Carolina Hurricanes, with Nicklas Lidstrom winning the Conn Smythe Trophy as the playoffs' MVP. Bowman and Hasek both retired after the season.

The 2003 season saw the Red Wings promote associate coach Dave Lewis to the head coach position after Bowman's retirement. Needing a new starting goaltender after Hasek's retirement, the Red wings signed Curtis Joseph from the Toronto Maple Leafs to a three year, $24 million deal. Also new to the lineup was highly touted Swedish prospect Henrik Zetterberg. The Red Wings finished the season second in the Western Conference and third overall in the NHL. The Red Wings were favored in their first round matchup against the 7th seeded Mighty Ducks of Anaheim. But the Ducks shocked the hockey world by sweeping the Red Wings in four games.

Longtime Wing Sergei Fedorov signed with the Mighty Ducks as a free agent during the offseason after a long contract dispute. Furthermore, Dominik Hasek decided to come out of retirement and joined the Wings for the 2003–04 season. Joseph, despite being one of the highest-paid players in the NHL, spent part of the season in the minor leagues, but after Hasek was sidelined for the season with an injury, Joseph led the team to the top of the Central Division and the league standings. The Red Wings eliminated the Nashville Predators in six games in the first round of the playoffs, which led to a second round matchup with the Calgary Flames. The Red Wings lost that game 1–0, and were eliminated the next game in Calgary by the same score in overtime.

During the 2004 offseason, the Wings focused on keeping players they already had instead of being active on the free agent market, resigning several players before the 2004–05 NHL lockout canceled the season.

2005 and beyond: New era for Detroit

On July 15, 2005, Mike Babcock, former head coach in Anaheim, became the new head coach for the Wings. During a November 21, 2005, game against the Nashville Predators, defenseman Jiri Fischer suffered a heart arrhythmia and collapsed on the bench. The game was canceled because of his injury, and was made up on January 23, 2006. This was the first time in NHL history a game had been postponed by injury. The game was played for the full 60 minutes; however, the Predators were allowed to maintain their 1–0 lead from the original game and won, 3–2. The Red Wings won the Presidents' Trophy with a 58–16–8 record, earning them 124 points.(NHL Standings [1]), and secured home ice advantage for the entire playoffs. The Wings opened the 2006 Stanley Cup playoffs against the Edmonton Oilers with a 3–2 overtime victory at Joe Louis Arena. However, the Oilers won 4 of the next 5 games to take the series.

Continuing the shakeup of the Red Wings roster, the offseason saw the departure of Brendan Shanahan and the return of Dominik Hasek, while Steve Yzerman announced his retirement after a 23-season Hall of Fame career with the Wings, having played the second most games in history (behind fellow Wing Alex Delvecchio) all with a single team. Yzerman further retired with the distinction of having been the longest serving team captain in NHL history.

The Red Wings opened the 2006–07 season with Nicklas Lidstrom as the new captain. The Red Wings retired Steve Yzerman's jersey number 19 on January 2. The Wings finished first in the Western Conference and tied for first in the NHL with the Buffalo Sabres, but the Sabres were awarded the Presidents' Trophy by virtue of having the greater number of wins. They advanced to the third round of the 2007 Stanley Cup playoffs after defeating the Calgary Flames and San Jose Sharks both in six games, coming back three straight after the Sharks' 2–1 series lead. The Red Wings lost to the eventual Stanley Cup winning team - the Anaheim Ducks, in the Western Conference Finals four games to two.

Nicklas Lidstrom, the current captain of the Wings

To start the 2007–08 campaign, Henrik Zetterberg recorded at least a point in each of Detroit's first 16 games, setting a club record. The Wings cruised to the playoffs, where they faced the Nashville Predators. After goalie Domenik Hasek played poorly in Games 3 and 4 of the series, both losses, head coach Mike Babcock replaced him with Chris Osgood. Osgood had departed the Wings earlier in the decade, only to be re-acquired as a backup in 2005. Osgood never left the net for the remainder of the playoffs, as the Red Wings came back in that series on their way to winning their eleventh Stanley Cup. The final victory came on June 4, 2008, against the Pittsburgh Penguins, by a score of 3-2. This was the Wings' fourth Stanley Cup in 11 years. Zetterberg scored the winning goal in the decisive Game 6, and was also named the winner of the Conn Smythe Trophy as the Most Valuable Player of the playoffs. It was the first time a team captained by a non-North American player (Nicklas Lidstrom) won the Stanley Cup.

On July 2, 2008, the Detroit Red Wings announced the signing of Marian Hossa. From the beginning of the 2008–09 season to New Year's Day, the Wings enjoyed success. Although they finished second in the conference to the San Jose Sharks, the Wings became the first team in NHL history to top 100 points in nine straight seasons. On January 1, 2009, the Red Wings played the Chicago Blackhawks in the third NHL Winter Classic at Chicago's Wrigley Field, beating them 6-4. The Wings entered the 2009 Stanley Cup Playoffs as the second overall seed in the Western Conference. The Red Wings handily swept the Columbus Blue Jackets, then beat the 8th-seeded Anaheim Ducks in a hard fought seven-game series. They took on the vastly improved Chicago Blackhawks in the Conference Finals, winning in five games. The Red Wings would face the Pittsburgh Penguins in the Finals for a second consecutive year, but this series would feature a different outcome. Pittsburgh defeated the Red Wings in seven games, Detroit becoming only the second NHL team to lose the Cup at home in Game 7.

The Red Wings began the 2009-10 NHL Season in Stockholm, Sweden, falling in both games to the St. Louis Blues by scores of 4-3 and 5-3, respectively. They were plagued by injuries throughout the season and lost the second most man-games to injury, with only the last place Edmonton Oilers losing more. The beginning of the season was a struggle for the Wings, with key players out of the lineup including Henrik Zetterberg, Tomas Holmstrom, Johan Franzen, Valtteri Filppula, and Niklas Kronwall. After the Olympic break, Detroit posted a record of 13-2-2 and earned 28 points, the most by any team in the NHL in the month of March. This run helped them secure the fifth playoff seed in the Western Conference, lengthening their streak of postseason appearances to 19 consecutive years, the longest current streak in all of North American professional sports.

Detroit won their first-round playoff series over the Phoenix Coyotes in seven games. In the second round, they fell behind the San Jose Sharks three games to one, before being knocked out of the playoffs in five games.

Team information

Uniforms

The Red Wings, like all NHL teams, updated their jerseys (traditionally known in hockey as "sweaters") to the new Rbk Edge standard for the 2007–08 NHL season. The Red Wings kept their design as close as possible, with a few exceptions: On the road (white) jersey, there is more red on the sleeves as the color panel begins closer to the shoulder. The white sleeve numbers on both jerseys were also moved up a bit, creating more red space between the bottom of the number and the wraparound white trim. The letters of the captain and alternate captains were moved to the player's right shoulder; Detroit is the only team in the league that made this change, although the 2008 NHL All Star jerseys featured this as well. All teams now have an NHL shield panel on the front of the jersey near the collar, and a rounded hemline at the bottom of the jersey which goes up at the hips, providing more mobility.

The Red Wings have not used any alternate logos or uniforms since the trend became popular in the 1990s, the sole exceptions were select games of the 1991–92 season commemorating the league's 75th Anniversary, and for a commemorative game in 1994 at Chicago Stadium. Those jerseys were based on the uniforms worn by the team (then the Detroit Cougars) in 1927–28. The throwbacks are primarily white with five red horizontal stripes on the body, the broadest middle stripe bearing "DETROIT" in bold letters, and three red stripes on the sleeves.

The striped throwbacks have been a popular design, as replicas continue to be marketed by the NHL. This jersey was also a basis for the uniforms worn by Wayne Gretzky's team of NHLPA All-Stars, nicknamed the "99ers", for their exhibition tour in Europe during the 1994–95 NHL lockout; a picture of Gretzky in this jersey was used for the cover art of a video game bearing his name.

Alternate jerseys for the RBK Edge system were made for 2008–2009 and continues today, but Detroit has thus far opted not to use alternates.

The Red Wings wore alternative "Retro" jerseys for the 2009 NHL Winter Classic in Chicago. The one-time jerseys were based on the uniforms worn by the then-Detroit Cougars during their inaugural season of 1926–27. These jerseys were white, with a single bold red stripe on the sleeves and chest, and a uniquely-styled white Old English "D" (a Detroit sports tradition, also currently used by the Detroit Tigers but formerly used by the Wings, Detroit Lions, and the University of Detroit Titans) centered on the chest stripe. These jerseys were also worn for their final 2009 regular season home game, again against the Chicago Blackhawks.

Fan traditions

Main article: Legend of the Octopus

The "Legend of the Octopus" is a sports tradition during Detroit Red Wings playoff games, in which an octopus is thrown onto the ice surface for good luck.

During the playoffs, Joe Louis Arena is generally adorned with a giant octopus with red eyes, nicknamed "Al" after Joe Louis Arena head ice manager Al Sobotka.

The 1952 playoffs featured the start of the tradition—the octopus throw. The owner of a local fish market, Peter Cusimano, threw one from the stands onto the ice. The eight legs were purportedly symbolic of the eight wins it took to win the Stanley Cup at the time. The Red Wings went on to sweep both of their opponents that year en route to a Stanley Cup championship. The NHL has, at various times, tried to eliminate this tradition but it continues to this day.

Al Sobotka is the man responsible for removing the thrown creatures from the ice. He is known for swinging the tossed octopuses above his head when walking off the ice. On April 19, 2008, NHL director of hockey operations Colin Campbell sent a memo to the Detroit Red Wings organization that forbids Zamboni drivers from cleaning up any octopuses thrown onto the ice and that violating the mandate would result in a $10,000 fine. Instead, it will be the linesmen who will perform this duty. In an email to the *Detroit Free Press*, NHL spokesman Frank Brown justified the ban because "matter flies off the octopus and gets on the ice" when Al Sobotka does it. This ban, however, was later loosened to allow for the octopus twirling to take place at the zamboni entrance.

During the late stages of games, especially around the end of the season and during the playoffs, the fans at Joe Louis Arena are known to start singing along to Journey's "Don't Stop Believin'". The lines, "born and raised in south Detroit" are the highlight of the song.

Broadcasters

The Red Wings' flagship radio stations are Detroit sister stations WXYT-AM 1270 and WXYT-FM 97.1. Games are carried on both stations unless there is a conflict with Detroit Lions football, Detroit Pistons basketball or Detroit Tigers baseball. There are several affiliate stations throughout Michigan, Northwestern Ohio, and Southwestern Ontario.

The Red Wings' exclusive local television rights are held by Fox Sports Detroit.

Announcers:

- Ken Daniels: Television Play by Play

- Mickey Redmond: Television Color Commentator (Home Games)
- John Keating: Television pre-game and post game show host
- Larry Murphy: Television Color Commentator / reporter
- Ken Kal: Radio Play by Play
- Paul Woods: Radio Analyst
- Trevor Thompson, Mickey York: TV pre-game and post-game show hosts / reporters

During many home games on FS Detroit where Ken Daniels and Mickey Redmond are in the booth, Larry Murphy also provides analysis "between the benches" during games. During road games which Mickey Redmond cannot attend, Murphy provides commentary alongside Daniels in the booth.

Hall of Fame broadcasters

Two members of the Red Wings organization have received the Foster Hewitt Memorial Award:

- Budd Lynch: TV and Radio Play by Play and Color - 1949-1975 (awarded 1985)
- Bruce Martyn: Radio Play by Play - 1964-1995 (awarded 1991)

Lynch called the first locally televised game at Olympia for the original WWJ-TV in 1949. He has remained with the organization for over 60 years, serving as Director of Publicity from 1975–1982, and public address announcer since 1982. Since 2008, John Fossen has joined Lynch in performing PA duties.

Season-by-season record

This is a partial list of the last five seasons completed by the Red Wings. For the full season-by-season history, see List of Detroit Red Wings seasons

Note: GP = Games played; W = Wins; L = Losses; T = Ties; OTL = Overtime losses; Pts = Points; GF = Goals for; GA = Goals against; PIM = Penalties in minutes

Records as of May 21, 2007.

Season	GP	W	L	OTL	Pts	GF	GA	PIM	Finish	Playoffs
2005–06	82	58	16	8	124	305	209	1127	1st, Central	Lost in Conference Quarterfinals, 2–4 (Oilers)
2006–07	82	50	19	13	113	254	199	982	1st, Central	Lost in Conference Finals, 2–4 (Ducks)
2007–08	82	54	21	7	115	257	184	937	1st, Central	Stanley Cup Champions, 4–2 (Penguins)
2008–09	82	51	21	10	112	295	244	824	1st, Central	Lost in **Finals**, 3–4 (Penguins)
2009–10	82	44	24	14	102	229	216	723	2nd, Central	Lost in Conference Semifinals, 1-4 (Sharks)

Notable players

Current roster

Updated October 12, 2010.

#	Nat	Player	Pos	S/G	Age	Acquired	Birthplace
8		Justin Abdelkader	C	L	24	2005	Muskegon, Michigan
44		Todd Bertuzzi	RW	L	36	2009	Sudbury, Ontario
11		Daniel Cleary	RW	L	32	2005	Carbonear, Newfoundland
13		Pavel Datsyuk (A)	C	L	32	1998	Sverdlovsk, Soviet Union
33		Kris Draper (A)	C	L	40	1993	Toronto, Ontario
17		Patrick Eaves	RW	R	27	2009	Calgary, Alberta
52		Jonathan Ericsson	D	L	27	2002	Karlskrona, Sweden
51		Valtteri Filppula	C	L	27	2002	Vantaa, Finland
93		Johan Franzen	LW	L	31	2004	Vetlanda, Sweden
43		Darren Helm	C	L	24	2005	St. Andrews, Manitoba
96		Tomas Holmstrom	RW	L	38	1994	Piteå, Sweden
35		Jimmy Howard	G	L	27	2003	Ogdensburg, New York
26		Jiri Hudler	LW	L	27	2002	Olomouc, Czechoslovakia
37		Doug Janik	D	L	31	2009	Agawam, Massachusetts
4		Jakub Kindl	D	L	24	2005	Šumperk, Czechoslovakia
55		Niklas Kronwall	D	L	30	2000	Stockholm, Sweden
5		Nicklas Lidstrom (C)	D	L	41	1989	Västerås, Sweden
20		Drew Miller	LW	L	27	2009	Dover, New Jersey
90		Mike Modano	C	L	41	2010	Livonia, Michigan
30		Chris Osgood	G	L	38	2005	Peace River, Alberta
28		Brian Rafalski	D	R	37	2007	Dearborn, Michigan
24		Ruslan Salei	D	L	36	2010	Minsk, Soviet Union
23		Brad Stuart	D	L	31	2008	Rocky Mountain House, Alberta
40		Henrik Zetterberg (A)	LW/C	L	30	1999	Njurunda, Sweden

Team captains

- Art Duncan, 1926–27
- Reg Noble, 1927–30
- George Hay, 1930–31
- Carson Cooper, 1931–32
- Larry Aurie, 1932–33
- Herbie Lewis, 1933–34
- Ebbie Goodfellow, 1934–35
- Doug Young, 1935–38
- Ebbie Goodfellow, 1938–42
- Sid Abel, 1942–43
- Mud Bruneteau, 1943–44
- William Hollett, 1944–46
- Sid Abel, 1946–52
- Ted Lindsay, 1952–56
- Red Kelly, 1956–58
- Gordie Howe, 1958–62
- Alex Delvecchio, 1962–73
- *Rotating captains*: Nick Libett, Red Berenson, Gary Bergman, Ted Harris, Mickey Redmond, & Larry Johnston, 1973–74
- Marcel Dionne, 1974–75
- Danny Grant, 1975–77
- Terry Harper, 1975–76
- Dennis Polonich, 1976–77
- Dan Maloney, 1977–78
- Dennis Hextall, 1978–79
- Nick Libett & Paul Woods, 1979 (co-captains)
- Dale McCourt, 1979–80
- Errol Thompson & Reed Larson, 1980–81 (co-captains)
- Reed Larson, 1981–82
- Danny Gare, 1982–86
- Steve Yzerman, 1986–2006
- Nicklas Lidstrom, 2006–*present*

Honored members

Hall of Famers:

Players (This is only a partial list as the Red Wings have 49 players enshrined which makes them third for all NHL teams. Only the Toronto Maple Leafs and Montreal Canadiens have more players in the Hall of Fame)

- Sid Abel, C/LW, 1938–1952, inducted 1969
- Marty Barry, C, 1935–1939, inducted 1965
- Andy Bathgate, RW, 1965–1967, inducted 1978
- Johnny Bucyk, LW, 1955–1957, inducted 1981
- Paul Coffey, D, 1993–1996, inducted 2004
- Roy Conacher, LW, 1946–1947, inducted 1998
- Alex Delvecchio, LW/C, 1951–1973, inducted 1977
- Marcel Dionne, C, 1971–1975, inducted 1992
- Viacheslav Fetisov, D, 1995–1998, inducted 2001
- Frank Fredrickson, C, 1926–1927 & 1930–1931, inducted 1958
- Bill Gadsby, D, 1961–1966, inducted 1970
- Eddie Giacomin, G, 1975–1978, inducted 1987
- Ebbie Goodfellow, D, 1929–1943, inducted 1963
- Doug Harvey, D, 1967, inducted 1973
- George Hay, LW, 1927–1931 & 1932–1933, inducted 1958
- Gordie Howe, RW, 1946–1971, inducted 1972
- Syd Howe, LW, 1934–1946, inducted 1965
- Brett Hull, RW, 2001–2004, inducted 2009
- Gordon "Duke" Keats, C, 1926–1927, inducted 1958
- Red Kelly, D/C, 1947–1960, inducted 1969
- Igor Larionov, C, 1995–2000, 2001–2003, inducted 2008
- Herbie Lewis, D, 1928–1939, inducted 1989
- Ted Lindsay, LW, 1944–1957, 1964–1965, inducted 1966
- Harry Lumley, G, 1944–1950, inducted 1980
- Larry Murphy, D, 1997–2001, inducted 2004
- Reg Noble, 1927–1932, inducted 1962
- Brad Park, D, 1983–1985, inducted 1988
- Marcel Pronovost, D, 1950–1967, inducted 1978
- Bill Quackenbush, D, 1942–1949, inducted 1976
- Luc Robitaille, LW, 2001–2003, inducted 2009
- Borje Salming, D, 1989–1990, inducted 1996
- Terry Sawchuk, G, 1949–1955, 1957–1964, 1968–69, inducted 1971

- Earl Seibert, D, 1943–1946, inducted 1963
- Darryl Sittler, C, 1984–1985, inducted 1989
- "Black" Jack Stewart, D, 1938–1950, inducted 1964
- Tiny Thompson, G, 1938–1940, inducted 1959
- Norm Ullman, C, 1955–1968, inducted 1982
- Steve Yzerman, C, 1983–2006, inducted 2009

Staff

- Jack Adams, Head coach, 1927–1947, inducted 1959
- Scotty Bowman, Head coach, 1993–2002, inducted in 1991
- Mike Ilitch, Owner, 1982–*present*, inducted 2003
- Tommy Ivan, Head coach, 1947–1954, inducted 1974

Numbers out of circulation

Retired jerseys:

- **1** Terry Sawchuk, G, 1949–55, 1957–64 & 1968–69, number retired March 6, 1994

- **7** Ted Lindsay, LW, 1944–57 & 1964–65, number retired November 10, 1991
- **9** Gordie Howe, RW, 1946–71, number retired March 12, 1972

The banners hanging at Joe Louis Arena.

- **10** Alex Delvecchio, C, 1950–73, number retired November 10, 1991
- **12** Sid Abel, LW, 1938–52, number retired April 29, 1995
- **19** Steve Yzerman, C, 1983–2006, number retired January 2, 2007 (the banner features the captain "C" to honor his tenure as the longest serving captain in NHL history)

Not available for issue:

- 6 Larry Aurie, RW, 1927–1939, following his retirement from the NHL. This was the first number ever retired by the Detroit Red Wings; however, Aurie does not have a banner hanging in Joe Louis Arena. The NHL's official information publication, the Official NHL Guide And Record Book, listed the number as being retired from 1975 until 2000 when reference to it was removed at the request of the Red Wings organization. The team no longer considers the number to be retired, although it is not available for use.
- 16 Vladimir Konstantinov, D, 1991–97, following a career-ending vehicular accident.

- 99 Wayne Gretzky, Although he was never a member of the Red Wings, his number was retired league-wide February 6, 2000

First-round draft picks

- 1963: Pete Mahovlich (2nd overall)
- 1964: Claude Gauthier (1st overall)
- 1965: George Forgie (3rd overall)
- 1966: Steve Atkinson (6th overall)
- 1967: Ron Barkwell (9th overall)
- 1968: Steve Andrascik (11th overall)
- 1969: Jim Rutherford (10th overall)
- 1970: Serge Lajeunesse (12th overall)
- 1971: Marcel Dionne (2nd overall)
- 1972: None (Pierre Guite 2nd round (26th overall))
- 1973: Terry Richardson (11th overall)
- 1974: Bill Lochead (9th overall)
- 1975: Rick Lapointe (5th overall)
- 1976: Fred Williams (4th overall)
- 1977: Dale McCourt (1st overall)
- 1978: Willie Huber (9th overall)
- 1979: Mike Foligno (3rd overall)
- 1980: Mike Blaisdell (11th overall)
- 1981: None (Claude Loiselle 2nd round (23rd overall)
- 1982: Murray Craven (17th overall)
- 1983: Steve Yzerman (4th overall)
- 1984: Shawn Burr (7th overall)
- 1985: Brent Fedyk (8th overall)
- 1986: Joe Murphy (1st overall)
- 1987: Yves Racine (11th overall)

- 1988: Kory Kocur (17th overall)
- 1989: Mike Sillinger (11th overall)
- 1990: Keith Primeau (3rd overall)
- 1991: Martin Lapointe (10th overall)
- 1992: Curtis Bowen (22nd overall)
- 1993: Anders Eriksson (22nd overall)
- 1994: Yan Golubovsky (23rd overall)
- 1995: Maxim Kuznetsov (26th overall)
- 1996: Jesse Wallin (26th overall)

- 1997: None (Yuri Butsayev 2nd round (49th overall))
- 1998: Jiri Fischer (25th overall)
- 1999: None (Jari Tolsa 4th round (120th overall))
- 2000: Niklas Kronwall (29th overall)
- 2001: None (Igor Grigorenko (62nd overall))
- 2002: None (Jiri Hudler 2nd round (58th overall))
- 2003: None (Jimmy Howard 2nd round (64th overall))
- 2004: None (Johan Franzen 3rd round (97th overall))
- 2005: Jakub Kindl (19th overall))
- 2006: None (Cory Emmerton 2nd round (41st overall))
- 2007: Brendan Smith (27th overall)
- 2008: Thomas McCollum (30th overall)
- 2009: None (Landon Ferraro (32nd overall))
- 2010: Riley Sheahan (21st overall)

Franchise scoring leaders

These are the top-ten point-scorers in franchise history. Figures are updated after each completed NHL regular season.

Note: *Pos = Position; GP = Games Played; G = Goals; A = Assists; Pts = Points; P/G = Points per game; * = current Red Wings player*

Points							Goals			Assists		
Player	Pos	GP	G	A	Pts	P/G	Player	Pos	G	Player	Pos	A
Gordie Howe	RW	1687	786	1023	1809	1.07	Gordie Howe	RW	786	Steve Yzerman	C	1063
Steve Yzerman	C	1514	692	1063	1755	1.16	Steve Yzerman	C	692	Gordie Howe	RW	1023
Alex Delvecchio	C	1549	456	825	1281	0.83	Alex Delvecchio	C	456	Alex Delvecchio	C	825
Nicklas Lidstrom*	D	1412	237	809	1046	0.74	Sergei Fedorov	C	400	Nicklas Lidstrom*	D	809
Sergei Fedorov	C	908	400	554	954	1.05	Ted Lindsay	LW	335	Sergei Fedorov	C	554
Norm Ullman	C	875	324	434	758	0.87	Norm Ullman	C	324	Norm Ullman	C	434
Ted Lindsay	LW	862	335	393	728	0.84	Brendan Shanahan	LW	309	Pavel Datsyuk*	C	394
Brendan Shanahan	LW	716	309	324	633	0.88	John Ogrodnick	RW	259	Ted Lindsay	LW	393
Pavel Datsyuk*	C	606	198	394	592	0.98	Nicklas Lidstrom*	D	237	Reed Larson	D	382
Reed Larson	D	708	188	382	564	0.80	Henrik Zetterberg*	C	206	Brendan Shanahan	LW	324

NHL awards and trophies

Stanley Cup

- 1935–36, 1936–37, 1942–43, 1949–50, 1951–52, 1953–54, 1954–55, 1996–97, 1997–98, 2001–02, 2007–08

Presidents' Trophy

- 1994–95, 1995–96, 2001–02, 2003–04, 2005–06, 2007–08

Clarence S. Campbell Bowl

- 1994–95, 1996–97, 1997–98, 2001–02, 2007–08, 2008–09

Prince of Wales Trophy

- 1935–36, 1936–37, 1942–43, 1949–50, 1950–51, 1951–52, 1952–53, 1953–54, 1954–55, 1956–57, 1964–65

Art Ross Trophy

- Ted Lindsay: 1949–50
- Gordie Howe: 1950–51, 1951–52, 1952–53, 1953–54, 1956–57, 1962–63

Bill Masterton Memorial Trophy

- Brad Park: 1983–84
- Steve Yzerman: 2003–04

Calder Memorial Trophy

- Jim McFadden: 1947–48
- Terry Sawchuk: 1950–51
- Glenn Hall: 1955–56
- Roger Crozier: 1964–65

King Clancy Memorial Trophy

- Brendan Shanahan: 2002–03

Lady Byng Memorial Trophy

- Marty Barry: 1936–37
- Bill Quackenbush: 1948–49
- Red Kelly: 1950–51, 1952–53, 1953–54
- Earl Reibel: 1955–56
- Alex Delvecchio: 1958–59, 1965–66, 1968–69
- Marcel Dionne: 1974–75
- Pavel Datsyuk: 2005–06, 2006–07, 2007–08, 2008–09

Lester B. Pearson Award

- Steve Yzerman: 1988–89
- Sergei Fedorov: 1993–94

Lester Patrick Trophy

- Jack Adams: 1965–66
- Gordie Howe: 1966–67
- Terry Sawchuk: 1970–71
- Alex Delvecchio: 1973–74
- Tommy Ivan and Bruce Norris: 1974–75
- Mike Ilitch: 1990–91
- Scotty Bowman: 2000–01
- Marcel Dionne: 2006–07
- Reed Larson: 2006–07
- Steve Yzerman: 2006–07

Conn Smythe Trophy

- Roger Crozier: 1965–66
- Mike Vernon: 1996–97
- Steve Yzerman: 1997–98
- Nicklas Lidstrom: 2001–02
- Henrik Zetterberg: 2007–08

Frank J. Selke Trophy

- Sergei Fedorov: 1993–94, 1995–96
- Steve Yzerman: 1999–00
- Kris Draper: 2003–04
- Pavel Datsyuk: 2007–08, 2008–09, 2009-10

Hart Memorial Trophy

- Ebbie Goodfellow: 1939–40
- Sid Abel: 1948–49
- Gordie Howe: 1951–52, 1952–53, 1956–57, 1957–58, 1959–60, 1962–63
- Sergei Fedorov: 1993–94

James Norris Memorial Trophy

- Red Kelly: 1953–54
- Paul Coffey: 1994–95
- Nicklas Lidstrom: 2000–01, 2001–02, 2002–03, 2005–06, 2006–07, 2007–08

Jack Adams Award

- Bobby Kromm: 1977–78
- Jacques Demers: 1986–87, 1987–88
- Scotty Bowman: 1995–96

NHL Plus/Minus Award

- Paul Ysebaert: 1991–92
- Vladimir Konstantinov: 1995–96
- Chris Chelios: 2001–02
- Pavel Datsyuk: 2007–08

Vezina Trophy

- Normie Smith: 1936–37
- Johnny Mowers: 1942–43
- Terry Sawchuk: 1951–52, 1952–53, 1954–55

William M. Jennings Trophy

- Chris Osgood and Mike Vernon: 1995–96
- Chris Osgood and Dominik Hasek: 2007–08

Mark Messier Leadership Award

- Chris Chelios: 2006–07

NHL All-Rookie Team

- 1984: Steve Yzerman
- 1991: Sergei Fedorov
- 1992: Nicklas Lidstrom and Vladimir Konstantinov
- 2003: Henrik Zetterberg
- 2010: Jimmy Howard

Franchise individual records

This is a partial list. For the more franchise records, see List of Detroit Red Wings records

- Most goals in a season: Steve Yzerman, 65 (1988–89)
- Most assists in a season: Steve Yzerman, 90 (1988–89)
- Most points in a season: Steve Yzerman, 155 (1988–89)
- Most penalty minutes in a season: Bob Probert, 398 (1987–88)
- Most points in a season, defenseman: Nicklas Lidstrom, 80 (2005–06)
- Most points in a season, rookie: Steve Yzerman, 87 (1983–84)
- Most wins in a season: Terry Sawchuk, 44 (1950–51 and 1951–52)
- Most shutouts in a season: Terry Sawchuk, 12 (1951–52, 1953–54, and 1954–55)
- Most shutouts in post-season: Dominik Hasek, 6 (2002)

See also

- Russian Five
- The Grind Line
- Victoria Cougars
- List of NHL players
- List of NHL seasons
- List of Stanley Cup champions

External links

- The Official website of the Detroit Red Wings [2]
  - List of Detroit Red Wings by number [3]

Transportation

Transportation in metropolitan Detroit

Transportation in metropolitan Detroit is provided by a comprehensive system of transit services, airports, and an advanced network of freeways which interconnect the city and region. The Michigan Department of Transportation (MDOT) administers the region's network of major roads and freeways. The region offers mass transit with bus services provided jointly by the Detroit Department of Transportation (DDOT) and the Suburban Mobility Authority for Regional Transportation (SMART) through a cooperative service and fare agreement. Cross border service between the downtown areas of Windsor and Detroit is provided by Transit Windsor via the Tunnel Bus. A monorail

Detroit Metropolitan Airport is the region's major international airport. The McNamara Terminal's ExpressTram is used to transport passengers from one end of the terminal to the other

system, known as the People Mover, operates daily through a 2.9 mile (4.6 km) loop in the downtown area. The Woodward Avenue Light Rail, beginning 2013, will serve as a link between the Detroit People Mover downtown and SEMCOG Commuter Rail with access to DDOT and SMART buses. Amtrak's current passenger facility is north of downtown in the New Center area. Amtrak provides service to Detroit, operating its *Wolverine* service between Chicago, Illinois, and Pontiac. Greyhound Bus operates a station on Howard Street near Michigan Avenue. The city's Dock and public terminal receives cruise ships on International Riverfront near the Renaissance Center which complements tourism in metropolitan Detroit.

Freeways

Main article: Roads and freeways in metropolitan Detroit

Metropolitan Detroit has a comprehensive network of interconnecting freeways including the I-75, the I-94 and the I-96 Interstate Highways. The region's extensive toll-free highway system which, together with its status as a major port city, provide advantages to its location as a global business center. There are no toll roads in Michigan. Taxi services and rental cars are readily available at the airport and throughout the metropolitan area.

Satellite image of the terminus at I-275.

Detroiters referred to their freeways by name rather than route number (Fisher Freeway and Crysler Freeway for sections of the I-75, Edsel Ford Freeway for a section of the I-94, Jeffries Freeway for parts of the I-96 and "The Lodge" for the M-10. M-53, while not officially designated, is commonly called the Van Dyke Expressway. Other freeways are referred to only by number as in the case of I-275 and M-59 with their names not being in common everyday usage. Detroit area freeways are sometimes sunken below ground level to permit local traffic to pass over the freeway.

The Detroit River International Crossing is a proposed new crossing linking I-75 and I-94 in the USA to Ontario Highway 401 in Canada avoiding the Ambassador Bridge. Proposed in 2004 it is yet to receive approval from the Michigan Senate.

Airports

Detroit Metropolitan Airport (DTW) is one of America's largest and most recently modernized facilities, with six major runways, Boeing 747 maintenance facilities, and an attached Westin Hotel and Conference Center. Located in nearby Romulus, DTW is metro Detroit's principal airport and is a hub for Delta Air Lines and Spirit Airlines. Bishop International Airport in Flint and Toledo Express Airport in Toledo, Ohio are other commercial passenger airports. Coleman A. Young International Airport (DET), commonly called Detroit City Airport, is on Detroit's northeast side, and offers charter service. Willow Run Airport in Ypsilanti primarily serves commercial aviation and offers charter services. Selfridge Air National Guard Base, a major military facility, is located in Mount Clemens. Smaller airports include Ann Arbor Municipal Airport (ARB), Oakland County International Airport (PTK) in Waterford Township which offers charter services, and St. Clair County International Airport near Port Huron, Michigan which serves as an international airport on the U.S. and Canadian Border.

Transit systems

Bus transportion

The Suburban Mobility Authority for Regional Transportation (SMART) is the public transit operator serving suburban portions of Metro Detroit which networks with the Detroit Department of Transportation (DDOT) serving the city of Detroit and the enclaves of Hamtramck and Highland Park. SMART and DDOT operate under a cooperative service and fare agreement. SMART maintains its administrative headquarters in the Buhl Building in downtown Detroit, while DDOT's major operations center is located at 1301 E. Warren

Detroit Amtrak Wolverine train.

Ave. in Detroit. As of 2008, SMART has the third highest ridership of Michigan's transit systems, surpassed by Capital Area Transportation Authority and Detroit Department of Transportation. Many of SMART's routes enter the City of Detroit and serve the Downtown and Midtown cores. Elsewhere in Detroit city limits, SMART policy does not permit passengers to be dropped off on outbound routes, or board on inbound routes. This is intended to avoid service duplication with Detroit Department of Transportation, which supplements the city of Detroit with its own bus service.

The Suburban Mobility Authority for Regional Transportation is the suburban bus system providing services outside the city, although SMART buses come in and out of the city on their routes. Visitors to the city can distinguish the two types of buses by their colors: DDOT buses have green and yellow stripes; SMART buses have red and orange stripes (both buses depicted on this page).

Greyhound Lines provides nation-wide service to the city of Detroit and the metropolitan area. Greyhound station is on Howard Street near Michigan Avenue.

Detroit People Mover

The Detroit People Mover is a 2.9-mile (4.7 km) monorail system which operates a loop encircling the central business district of downtown Detroit. The city's monorail system, known as the People Mover is run by the Detroit Transportation Corporation of the City of Detroit.

Intercity rail

Intercity rail services using the Wolverine line are available from Detroit (Amtrak station) offering service to Chicago, Illinois, Pontiac and intermediate stations. Infrastructure work is in progress to improve journey times on this line.

Woodward Light Rail

The Woodward Avenue Light Rail is a proposed light rail system that would run along Woodward Avenue from downtown to the 8 Mile Road serving Wayne State University, Detroit's New Center and Detroit (Amtrak station). From the railway station it would connect to Ann Arbor using the SEMCOG Commuter Rail and to Chicago using the Chicago–Pontiac–Detroit high speed rail project.

The cost of the light rail system is estimated as $372 million with a plan to begin operation by 2013.

A private group of Detroit area investors has provided matching funds to government dollars to developing a $125 million, 3.4 mile line through central Detroit (similar to the Tacoma Link) called the *M-1 Rail Line*. The proposed line received $25 million in funding from the United States Department of Transportation in February 2010. Groundbreaking is scheduled to begin at the end of 2010. City, State, and Federal officials are developing a plan to for a nine mile extension to continue M-1 Rail Line to 8 Mile Rd. along Woodward Avenue. The DDOT proposal estimates daily ridership at 22,000 by 2015.

SEMCOG Commuter Rail

SEMCOG Commuter Rail is a proposed regional rail link between the cities of Ann Arbor and Detroit which is currently 'on hold'. Previously an October 2010 completion had been suggested. The stops includes new or existing stations in Ann Arbor, Detroit Metropolitan Airport, Ypsilanti, The Henry Ford, Dearborn, and Detroit's New Center area. The route would extend 38.5 miles (62.0 km) from Ann Arbor to Detroit, along the same route used by Amtrak's *Wolverine*. The planned system has secured $100 million in federal grants.

Bicycling

Main article: Cycling in Detroit

Like many American cities, Detroit embraced bicycling during the "golden age" of the 1890s. However, as the automotive era began, the interests of bicycle shop owners, manufacturers, racers, and enthusiasts turned to the automobile.

Now, Detroiters are rediscovering the bicycle, helped in part by significant infrastructure investments as well as bicycle-friendly and extensive road infrastructure.

Commercial freight

Further information: Economy of metropolitan Detroit

History

1805-1928

The period from 1800 to 1929 was one of considerable growth of the city, from 1,800 people in 1820 to 1,560,000 in 1930 (2,300,000 for the metropolitan area). During this period a new road system had been created in 1805, a regional rail network was constructed, a thriving streetcar network developed and an emerging global motorcar industry was established in the city.

In 1805 five new radial avenues (Woodward, Michigan, Grand River, Gratiot, and Jefferson) were constructed in the city as part of a new city plan drawn up by Augustus Woodward following a devastating fire in the city earlier the same year.

Over land the Sauk Trail, a Native American trail which ran through Michigan, Illinois and Indiana connected Detroit with Sauk Village, Illinois and Chicago; in 1820 it was described as a 'plain horse path, which is considerably traveled by traders, hunters, and others' but one which not possible for someone unfamiliar with the route to follow without a guide.

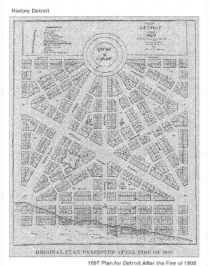

History Detroit

1807 Plan for Detroit After the Fire of 1805

Augustus Woodward's plan following the 1805 fire for Detroit's baroque styled radial avenues and Grand Circus Park.

Congress passed an act to construct a new Chicago Road from Detroit to supply Fort Dearborn in Chicago, surveying began in 1825 however financial shortfalls resulted in the road mostly following the path of the Sauk Trail which military couriers were already using. By 1835, daily stage coach departures run by the Western Stage Company traveled all the way from Chicago to Detroit on a multi-day trip whose travel time was dependent on how bad the road was at the particular season.

The Erie Canal, which had first be proposed in 1807, opened in 1825 and greatly improved access to Detroit and other Michigan ports from Europe and the eastern seaboard. From Detoit settles were able to use the Chicago Road and other land routes. Land sales in Detroit reached a peak in that year with 92,232 acres being sold.

A charter for the Detroit and Pontiac Railroad was granted in 1830 to link Detroit with Pontiac however it was not until 1843 that the line was completed and operation started from a station at Jefferson & Woodward Avenue. Plans for a railway line to St. Joseph, Michigan and then on to

Chicago by boat wereoutlined in 1930, and after a number of funding problem the line reached Dexter ten years later and Kalamazoo, Michigan in 1846 when the Michigan Central Railroad was formed to progress the work faster and replace faulty rails that had already installed. The new company decided to create a line all the way to Chicago (via New Buffalo rather than St. Joseph) which they completed by 1852.

An ordinance was passed in May 1863 awarded a 30 year franchise to the *Detroit City Railway Company* for the construction of horse drawn streetcar system in the city; construction started in June and services were available to the public from late August. By the end of the year services were operating along Jefferson, Woodward, Gratiot and Michigan. Other companies were also established on other streets and business was brisk, by 1875; the Detroit City Railway Company alone carried 2,900,000 passengers on their four lines. The first electric streecars started operation in 1886 and the last horse drawn trams in 1895. In 1880 the Grand Trunk Western Railroad was formed to provide a new route to Chicago through lower Michigan.

Work started on the construction of the 12 mile long U-shaped Grand Boulevard road around the city in 1891 which was completed in 1913. The entire length was decorated with trees, shrubbery, and flowerbeds.

Henry Ford tested his new Quadricycle, gasoline-powered motor car, in Detroit on 4 June 1896.

The Detroit and Toledo Shore Line Railroad which linked Detroit with Toledo, Ohio opened in 1903. The Detroit, Toledo and Ironton Railroad was formed in 1905 from the merger of two existing companies, it went bankrupt in 1908 but remained solvent and was later bought by Henry Ford in 1920 to carry raw materials and finished goods to and from his factories in Dearborn, Michigan.

The Michigan Central Railway Tunnel between Detroit and Canada opened in 1910 followed by Michigan Central Station in 1913 after a fire at the previous station. The New York State Barge Canal opened in 1918 offering a improved route route to the Eastern seaboard compared to the Erie Canal. The Ford Airport (Dearborn) opened in 1924 which added an Airship mooring mast in the following year. The Ford River Rouge Complex was completed in 1928 by which time it was the largest integrated factory with some 100,000 employees during the 1930s.

1929-1969

The years following the Wall Street Crash of 1929 until 1969 saw the creation of the Interstate Highway System, rapid growth of the suburbs and associated shopping malls, the growing importance of civil aviation and growing dominance of the motorcar; it also witnessed the end of the streetcar system in the city followed by an increased use of buses. The 1967 Detroit riot only accelerated rate at which people, mainly white, were moving to the suburbs, with some 88,000 leaving in 1968 alone. The city population peaked at 1.85 million in 1950 before falling to 1.5 million in 1970; the metropolitan area's population peaked in 1970 at 4.5 million. There was growing opposition to urban freeway construction in many cities across the US, including Detroit, in the 1960s and the city authorities modified, scaled back and cancelled a number of schemes and passed a decree stating that no further urban freeways would be constructed in the city.

The Ambassador Bridge, a road bridge to Canada, opened in 1929 and then the Detroit–Windsor road tunnel in 1930 which was also the year of the first flight from Detroit Metropolitan Wayne County Airport. By the late 1920s railroad-highway intersections were becoming a creating serious travel delays and accidents. The railway companies agreed to contribute half the $2million cost of creating a number of grade separated junctions; the Michigan Central Railway, Pennsylvania railroad and Wabash Railway contributed $200,000 towards the ambitious 204-foot (62 m) Fort Street-Pleasant Street and Norfolk & Western Railroad Viaduct which opened in 1930. This work was undertaken when Fort Street close to the Ford River Rouge Complex was converted to a 'superhighway' with a divided highway an night-time lighting.

By 1934 the general manager of the Detroit Streetcar Railway, Fred A. Nolan, was campaigning to convert the Detroit streetcars to all buses within 20 years.

The City of Detroit owned the streetcar system starting in 1922, one of the first transit systems to be publicly owned in the US, as the Department of Street Railways. The DSR was run by the three man Detroit Street Railways Commission that was appointed by the mayor of Detroit. The public ownership of the DSR remained until its end on July 1, 1974, long after streetcar service ended on April 8, 1957.

Approval was given in 1940 for the Davison Freeway which was the nation's first urban depressed highway; the six-lane limited-access highway opened in 1942. In 1941 the Willow run bypass was rapidly constructed as a four-lane divided highway following the attack on Pearl Harbor to bring workers from Detroit to the Willow Run factory to the west of the city where Henry Ford had constructed a factory to produce the B-24 Liberator military aircraft.

By 1945, prepared plans included trains running within the median strips with of a complex expressway and subway system in the city. The Ford airport closed in 1947 when all remaining services were transferred to Wayne County. In 1949 National City Lines was found guilty of attempting to monopolise the sector by the supreme court in what became known as the Great American streetcar scandal.

The first major discontinued use of street rail occurred on Grand River on May 5, 1947 to alleviate rush hour congestion. In September 1951 the Grand River line was converted to Trolley Coach operations, an experiment that would last until November 1962 when the line was replaced by diesel buses. General Manager of the DSR, Leo J. Nowicki, justified discontinued use of rail on Jefferson Ave in January 1954, citing that the cost of replacing worn out track and maintaining overhead wires would cost around $1,647,500 while the cost of purchasing 40 new 51-passenger diesel buses would only cost around $800,000. On February 7 the Jefferson line was replaced by buses followed by the Michigan-Gratiot line on September 7, 1955. By 1956 only the Gratiot and Woodward line remained. On September 12, 1955 the Detroit Street Railway Commission approved the replacement of Detroit's last streetcar rout for the spring of 1956. The commission argued that replacing streetcars with buses would allow more flexibility in rout scheduling; eliminate mid street loading zones and allow curbside passenger pick up, increasing safety; and reduce operating cost.

In 1950 both Pan-Am and BOAC started services from Detroit Metropolitan Wayne County Airport. Also in 1950 GM Truck & Coach introduced new 40-foot-long (12 m) diesel-powered transit coach and during 1951 the Mt. Elliott, Oakland, Trumbull, Clairmount, and Mack lines were converted from streetcars to buses. Streetcar ridership had declined after World War II and a protracted union conflict over single-man operation of a new generation of streetcars included a damaging 59 day strike during 1951. A decision on the future of streetcars in Detroit gained urgency with the nearing completion of the Edsel Ford Freeway as part of which the Detroit Street Railway Commission was expected to pay $70,000 to support streetcar operation over the new Gratiot Avenue Bridge. The Edsel Ford Freeway and The Lodge were completed in the 1950s

Northland Center, one of four new suburban shopping malls (the others were Eastland Center, Southland Center, and Westland Center) which opened 1954 was built by J. L. Hudson Company, a major upscale Detroit based department store chain. The Jefferson Avenue line streetcar line was converted to buses in 1954, then the Michigan Avenue in line 1955, Gratiot Avenue in March 1956 and Woodward Avenue two weeks later. An "End of the Line" grand parade and final excursion along Woodward Avenue was held on April 8, 1956. By late 1955 some 186 of Detroit's streetcars had been sold to Mexico City.

The Saint Lawrence Seaway opened in 1959 allowing ocean going ships to access the Great Lakes and Detroit. The Fisher Freeway was built in the 'early 1960s' and the Chrysler Freeway in 1967 (both of which are now part of the I-75). In 1968 the Davison Freeway was extended a few blocks through a junction with the newly opened Chrysler Freeway.

The new Jeffries Freeway (I-96) was intended to have followed the route of Grand River Avenue however led to opposition as were many other schemes across the country.

1970-present

In the 1970s the Jeffries Freeway was completed, followed by a number of transit schemes and pedestrian/cycling schemes. The population of the city fell from 1,500,000 in 1970 to 910,000 in 2009; since 1970 the population of the metropolitan area has fallen by 100,000.

The modified Jeffries freeway opened in stages in 1970, 1971 and 1972 with further elements being added between 1973 and 1977.

In 1976 a one mile narrow-gauge heritage trolley bus service along an "L-shaped" route from Grand Circus Park to the Renaissance Center along Washington Boulevard and Jefferson Avenue, with the trams coming from Lisbon, Portugal. The tram was originally just 3/4 miles long, but was extended 1/4 mile to the Renaissance Center in 1980.

The Detroit People Mover opened in 1987 after some 20 years of discussion. In 1988 Michigan Central Station closed and passenger services were moved to the Detroit (Amtrak station) in the New Center, Detroit area.

The William G. Milliken State Park and Harbor which included a 52 berth marina opened in 2003; the park was then extended in 2009.

Washington Boulevard was refurbished in 2003 and the heritage narrow-gauge trolley-bus service was closed at the same time (the service had lost of most of its patronage following the opening of the People Mover).

3.5 miles (5.6 km) of continuous RiverWalk along the Detroit International Riverfront between the Ambasdor Bridge and Belle Isle and two of four planned pavilions opened in 2007. A further section of the riverwalk from the Ambassador Bridge to the River Rouge is not expected to open before 2012.

In 2009 the approach to the Ambassador Bridge from the US side was redesigned to provide a direct access to the bridge from I-96 and I-75. In the same year a 1.2 miles (1.9 km) section of the Dequindre Cut, a cycle and greenway from Gratiot Avenue south to Woodbridge Street, between Jefferson Avenue and the Detroit River; extensions are planned north to Mack Avenue and south to the William G. Milliken State Park and Harbor. The 'Detroit Non-Motorized Master Plan' was also published which proposed 400 miles of bike lanes primarily through road diets. The Rosa Parks bus terminal opened.

In 2010 the new 407-foot-long Bagley Avenue Pedestrian Bridge re-connected Mexicantown bridging both I-75 and I-96.

See also

- Detroit River
- Detroit–Windsor
- Great Lakes Waterway
- Tourism in metropolitan Detroit

Further reading

- Building Autopia: The Development of Urban Freeway Planning in the Pre-Interstate Era [1]

Big Beaver Airport

The **Big Beaver Airport**, formerly (IATA: **3BB**), was a small suburban general aviation airport located at the corners of Big Beaver Road and John R Road in Troy, MichiganGeographical coordinates: 42°33′53″N 83°06′30″W

.

It was created in 1946 as an auxiliary airfield with a 2,400 ft (220 m²) gravel runway. By the 1970's, the main airstrip was converted to asphalt and a 2,100 ft (200 m²) sod runway was added. Flight training was done in Aeronca 7AC and Cessna 150/152 aircraft. Rentals later included a Piper PA23, Cessna 172 Skyhawks and a Cessna 172RG Cutlass. The airfield closed around 1995. originally the John Main family farm, it was owned and operated by his surviving daughter, Miss Anna Main, until her death. As she was never married and had no children, the city of Troy reached an agreement to let her operate the field until she died, at which time the city would acquire the property.[1]

The airfield has since been developed into various office buildings and small industrial centers.

External links

- Abandoned & Little Known Airfields of Michigan [2]

Oakland-Troy Airport

Geographical coordinates: 42°32′35″N 083°10′40″W

Oakland/Troy Airport		
IATA: *none* – ICAO: KVLL – FAA LID: VLL		
Summary		
Airport type	Public	
Owner	Oakland County	
Serves	Troy, Michigan	
Hub for	{{{hub}}}	
Elevation AMSL	729 ft / 222 m	
Coordinates	{{{coordinates}}}	
Runways		
Direction	**Length**	**Surface**
	ft	**m**	
9/27	3,550	1,082	Asphalt
Statistics (2006)		
Aircraft operations		32,466
Source: Federal Aviation Administration		

Oakland/Troy Airport (ICAO: **KVLL**, FAA LID: **VLL**) is a county-owned public-use airport located two miles (3 km) east of the central business district of Troy, a city in Oakland County, Michigan, United States.

The Oakland/Troy Airport is considered the county's 'executive' airport. Business travelers and tourists using private, corporate and charter aircraft benefit from the airport's convenient proximity to business, recreation and entertainment facilities. It is located between Maple Road and 14 Mile Road and Coolidge Highway and Crooks Road.

Although most U.S. airports use the same three-letter location identifier for the FAA and IATA, Oakland/Troy Airport is assigned **VLL** by the FAA but has no designation from the IATA (which assigned **VLL** to Valladolid, Spain).

Facilities and aircraft

Oakland/Troy Airport covers an area of 119 acres (48 ha) which contains one runway designated 9/27 with a 3,550 x 60 ft (1,082 x 18 m) asphalt pavement. For the 12-month period ending December 31, 2006, the airport had 32,466 general aviation aircraft operations, an average of 88 per day.

Charter passenger, air freight, as well as aircraft maintenance and fuel, are available on the field.

Other Airport Information: There are currently 108 aircraft based at Oakland/Troy Airport.

Single Engined Aircraft: 95
Multi Engined Aircraft: 10
Helicopters: 3
Jets: 0
(On occasion, a small jet may visit the airport)

External links

- Resources for this airport:
  - AirNav airport information for KVLL [1]
  - FlightAware airport information [2] and live flight tracker [3]
  - NOAA/NWS latest weather observations [4]
  - SkyVector aeronautical chart [5], Terminal Procedures [6] for KVLL

Interstate 75

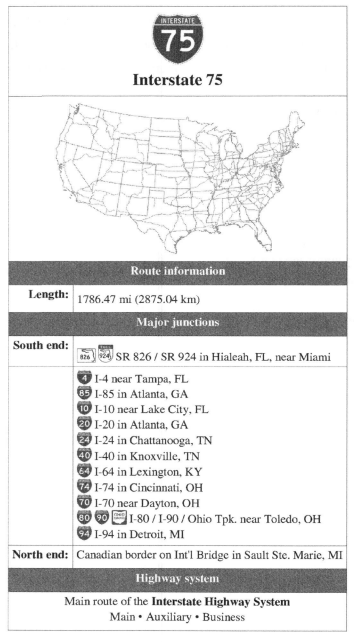

Interstate 75

Route information	
Length:	1786.47 mi (2875.04 km)
Major junctions	
South end:	SR 826 / SR 924 in Hialeah, FL, near Miami
	I-4 near Tampa, FL
	I-85 in Atlanta, GA
	I-10 near Lake City, FL
	I-20 in Atlanta, GA
	I-24 in Chattanooga, TN
	I-40 in Knoxville, TN
	I-64 in Lexington, KY
	I-74 in Cincinnati, OH
	I-70 near Dayton, OH
	I-80 / I-90 / Ohio Tpk. near Toledo, OH
	I-94 in Detroit, MI
North end:	Canadian border on Int'l Bridge in Sault Ste. Marie, MI
Highway system	
Main route of the **Interstate Highway System** Main • Auxiliary • Business	

Interstate 75 (**I-75**) is a major north–south Interstate Highway in the Great Lakes and Southeastern regions of the United States. It travels from State Road 826 (Palmetto Expressway) and State Road 924

(Gratigny Parkway) in Hialeah, Florida (northwest of Miami) to Sault Ste. Marie, Michigan, at the Ontario, Canada, border. Interstate 75 passes through six different states: Florida, Georgia, Tennessee, Kentucky, Ohio and Michigan.

Route description

Lengths

	mi	km
FL	470.88	757.81
GA	355.11	571.49
TN	161.86	260.49
KY	191.78	308.64
OH	211.30	340.05
MI	395.54	636.56
Total	1786.47	2875.04

Florida

Main article: Interstate 75 in Florida

Interstate 75 begins its northerly journey at an interchange with State Road 924 and State Road 826 in Hialeah, a suburb of Miami. After an intersection with the Homestead Extension of Florida's Turnpike and an interchange with Interstate 595 and the Sawgrass Expressway, the interstate leaves the Miami metropolitan area and turns westward to travel through the Everglades along the tolled Alligator Alley, which brings the highway to the Gulf Coast and Naples, where it again heads north. Passing through Bonita Springs, Fort Myers, and Sarasota, Interstate 75 encounters a series of construction projects that will increase the lane count from two lanes in each direction to three in each direction. The freeway enters the Tampa Bay metropolitan area before the interchange with Interstate 275 northbound, which handles St. Petersburg-bound traffic. Within the Tampa metro are three more major junctions: One with the Lee Roy Selmon Crosstown Expressway which carries traffic into downtown Tampa; one with Interstate 4 which carries traffic across the center of the state to the East Coast; and another as Interstate 275 traffic defaults back onto northbound. The freeway proceeds to enter suburban portions of Pasco, Hernando, and Sumter counties on its way to Ocala and Gainesville. At Lake City, Florida, the Christopher Columbus Transcontinental Highway, Interstate 10, intersects with Interstate 75, providing routes toward Jacksonville, Florida; Tallahassee; Mobile, Alabama; and points westward. Afterward, the northmost stetch of Interstate 75 in Florida exits the Sunshine State into southern

Georgia.

Georgia

Main article: Interstate 75 in Georgia

Interstate 75 enters Georgia near Valdosta, and it continues northward through the towns of Tifton and Cordele until it reaches the Macon area, where it intersects with Interstate 16 eastbound towards Savannah. For northbound traffic wishing to avoid potential congestion in Macon, Interstate 475 provides a relatively straight bypass west of that city and Interstate 75's route. After Macon it passes the small town of Forsyth. The freeway reaches no major junctions again until in the Atlanta metropolitan area. The first metropolitan freeway met is Interstate 675, then followed by the Atlanta "Perimeter" bypass, Interstate 285. It crosses inside the Perimeter and heads northeast several miles towards the Atlanta city center. Interstate 75 is then duplexed with Interstate 85 due north through the central business district of Atlanta. After the two Interstates split, Interstate 75 makes a beeline northwest, crossing outside the Interstate 285 Perimeter and heading towards the major suburban city of Marietta. This section of Interstate 75 just north of Interstate 285 has 15 through lanes, making it the widest roadway anywhere in the Interstate Highway System.. North of Marietta, the final major junction in the Atlanta metropolitan area is the Interstate 575 spur. Interstate 75 then traverses the hilly northwestern Georgia terrain as it travels towards Chattanooga, Tennessee.

Tennessee

Main article: Interstate 75 in Tennessee

The freeway enters Tennessee directly in the Chattanooga metropolitan area, where it intersects with Interstate 24. Exiting Chattanooga to the northeast, Interstate 75 passes through an area known for dense fog. Twelve people were killed and 42 were injured in a 99 vehicle accident on that stretch of I-75 in heavy fog on December 11, 1990. Interstate 75 does not meet any other highways until it is multiplexed with Interstate 40 and heads eastbound. Together, they enter the outskirts of Knoxville, where Interstate 75 multiplexes itself with a different road, this time Interstate 640, but only for a short time. When the two meet Interstate 275, Interstate 75 becomes its own freeway and heads north towards the Kentucky border. On the journey northward from Knoxville to the Kentucky border, interstate 75 encounters some of its highest points of elevation through the Cumberland Mountains and Cumberland Plateau region, cutting through the uppermost peaks and ridges of the mountains.

Kentucky

Main article: Interstate 75 in Kentucky

Interstate 75 continues northbound through the hilly and rugged terrain of the Cumberland Plateau region of Kentucky passing through London, KY and Richmond, KY eventually reaching Lexington, where it briefly runs coterminiously with Interstate 64 before splitting off for Cincinnati, Ohio. Near Walton, Interstate 71 merges with Interstate 75, making for yet another multiplexed portion of freeway. Interstate 275, which is the Cincinnati beltway, is then intersected by Interstate 71/75. After passing through Covington, the freeway crosses the Ohio River via the lower level of the Brent Spence Bridge and continues into Cincinnati.

Ohio

Main article: Interstate 75 in Ohio

Immediately after entering Cincinnati, Interstate 71 separates from Interstate 75, taking a more easterly routing through the city, while Interstate 75 remains generally northbound throughout the metropolitan area. Interstate 74 westbound, Ohio State Route 562 eastbound, and Ohio State Route 126 all intersect the freeway as it makes its way northward. In Arlington Heights, a suburb of Cincinnati, Interstate 75 sees a carriageway split for a few miles. After another interchange with the Interstate 275 beltway, the freeway continues in the metropolitan area, passes through Middletown and heads towards Dayton, where Interstate 675 and Interstate 70 have interchanges. After exiting Dayton, Interstate 75 makes its way northbound through Ohio, passing through the smaller cities of Lima, Findlay and Bowling Green before finally reaching Toledo, located on the Michigan border. Interstate 475 is met first south of the city, and then the cross-country highways of Interstate 80/Interstate 90/Ohio Turnpike. Interstate 475 then meets with 75 again. Interstate 280 is the last major junction in Ohio; the freeway crosses into Michigan soon afterwards.

Mackinac Bridge

Michigan

Main article: Interstate 75 in Michigan

Interstate 75 hugs the western shore of Lake Erie upon entering Michigan—until about Monroe, when it heads westward and prepares to enter Detroit and its surrounding suburbs. Yet another I-275 is met as the freeway goes deeper into the Detroit metropolitan area, and no other major junctions are present until downtown. Once downtown, Interstate 75 meets the Ambassador Bridge to Windsor, Ontario, Interstate 375 (Chrysler Freeway), I-94, I-96, M-10 and M-8 (Davison Freeway).

I-696 also intersects I-75 in the northern metro area. When the freeway reaches Pontiac, there is a junction with M-59; and further north in Flint, the interstate meets I-475 and I-69. The freeway then heads north towards Saginaw, where I-675 acts as a spur route into the city. Further north in Bay City, the major junction of US 10 exists, providing access to Midland as well as downtown Bay City. The last major interchange occurs at 4 Mile Road just south of Grayling where US 127 northbound ends with traffic merging onto northbound I-75 and the southbound starts taking drivers through the center of the state granting easier access to cities such as Clare, Mt. Pleasant, Lansing, and Jackson. At Mackinaw City, I-75 crosses the Mackinac Bridge to reach the Upper Peninsula. It is the only Interstate located in the Upper Peninsula of Michigan, and it continues to where the road terminates at the Canadian border in Sault Ste. Marie.

On the Canadian side, drivers must use a series of city streets in Sault Ste. Marie, Ontario to reach Highway 17, the local route of the Trans-Canada Highway.

History

This limited access highway that was planned in the 1950s roughly follows the general route of many older at-grade highways, including U.S. Route 2, U.S. Route 27, U.S. Route 25, and U.S. Route 41, among others. Some of these older U.S. Routes (several of which are still in existence) previously had replaced the eastern route of the old *Dixie Highway*.

Interstate 75 was intended to end at Tampa in the original interstate highway plans. However, vast population growth in southwestern Florida (e.g. Ft. Myers, Naples, etc.) and a desire to link the Tampa Bay Area with South Florida, called for a new expressway artery. At first, Florida state legislators proposed a toll in the corridor, but by 1968, it was cancelled in favor of the extension of I-75 southwards. Next, it was decided to link I-75 from Naples to South Florida with an upgraded version of an existing private toll road, the Alligator Alley, and then connect it with Interstate 95 in North Miami, although due to local opposition, I-75 ends a few miles short of I-95.

On December 21, 1977, I-75 was complete from Tampa to Sault Ste. Marie with a segment opening north of Marietta, Georgia. The final stretch of Interstate 75 was completed in 1986 in Dade (present Miami-Dade) and Broward Counties in Florida, but the last stretch to receive the I-75 signage was a reconstructed (rebuilt with more lanes) Alligator Alley on November 25, 1992.

On July 15, 2009, a fuel tanker exploded under an overpass on 9 Mile Road in Hazel Park resulting in the overpass collapsing onto I-75.

Major intersections

- Homestead Extension of Florida's Turnpike near Miami Lakes, Florida (southbound exit and northbound entrance)
- Interstate 595 in Davie, Florida, serving Fort Lauderdale-Hollywood International Airport
- Interstate 275 near Parrish, Florida
- Florida State Road 60 near Brandon, Florida
- Interstate 4 near Tampa, Florida
- Interstate 275 near Lutz, Florida
- Interstate 10 in Lake City, Florida
- Interstate 475 around Macon, Georgia (twice).
- Interstate 16 in Macon, Georgia (**Map** [1])
- Interstate 675 near Stockbridge, Georgia
- Interstate 285 outside Atlanta (loop around the city), on the southeast side in Clayton County and on the northwest side near Marietta
- Interstate 85 in Atlanta. They stay connected for several miles through downtown on a highway known as the Downtown Connector.
- Interstate 20 in Atlanta
- Interstate 24 in Chattanooga, Tennessee
- Interstate 40 near Lenoir City, Tennessee. They stay connected until Knoxville, Tennessee.
- Interstate 64 in Lexington, Kentucky. They stay connected for 6 miles (9.7 km) to the east of downtown Lexington.
- Interstate 71 in Walton, Kentucky. They stay connected until Cincinnati, Ohio.
- Interstate 275 in Erlanger, Kentucky (loop around Cincinnati), and again in Sharonville, Ohio
- Interstate 74 in Cincinnati
- Interstate 675 in Miamisburg, Ohio (south of Dayton)
- Interstate 70 in Vandalia, Ohio (near Dayton)
- Interstate 80 / 90 (Ohio Turnpike) in Rossford, Ohio (near Toledo)
- Interstate 475 in Perrysburg and Toledo, Ohio
- Interstate 280 in Toledo, Ohio
- Interstate 275 in Newport, Michigan
- Interstate 96 (Jeffries Freeway) in Detroit, Michigan
- M-10 (Lodge Freeway) in Detroit
- Interstate 375 in Detroit
- Interstate 94 (Ford Freeway) in Detroit
- M-8 (Davison Freeway) in Detroit
- Interstate 696 (Walter P. Reuther Freeway) north of Detroit

I-75 co-signed with I-85 in midtown Atlanta

- Interstate 69 in Flint, Michigan
- Interstate 475 in Flint
- Interstate 675 in Saginaw, Michigan
- US 10 west of Bay City, Michigan

Auxiliary routes

- Tampa, Florida/St. Petersburg, Florida - I-175 (1.294 mi/2.08 km), I-275 (63.387 mi/102.01 km), I-375 (1.220 mi/1.96 km)
- Macon, Georgia - I-475
- Atlanta, Georgia - I-675
- Suburban Spur to Canton, Georgia, I-575 in the Atlanta area
- Knoxville, Tennessee - I-275
- Knoxville, Tennessee - I-640
- Cincinnati, Ohio - I-275
- Dayton, Ohio - I-675
- Toledo, Ohio - I-475
- Detroit, Michigan - I-275, I-375
- Flint, Michigan - I-475
- Saginaw, Michigan - I-675

References

- 2005 Rand McNally Road Atlas
- FDOT [1] GIS data and pavement management reports [2]
- Georgia Department of Transportation, Office of Transportation Data (2003). *Interstate Mileage Report (438 Report)* [3].

External links

- Interstate 75 [4] at Michigan Highways
- Interstate 75 [5] on Cincinnati-Transit.net

Main US Interstate Highways (major interstates highlighted)																		
4	5	8	10	12	15	16	17	19	20	22	24	25	26	27	29	30		
35	37	39	40	43	44	45	49	55	57	59	64	65	66	68	69			
70	71	72	73	74	75	76 (W)		76 (E)		77	78	79	80	81	82			
83	84 (W)		84 (E)		85	86 (W)		86 (E)		87	88 (W)		88 (E)		89	90		
91	93	94	95	96	97	99	(238)		H-1		H-2		H-3					
Unsigned			A-1		A-2		A-3		A-4		PRI-1		PRI-2		PRI-3			
Lists	Primary		Main - Intrastate - Suffixed - Future - Gaps															
	Auxiliary		Main - Future - Unsigned															
	Other		Standards - Business - Bypassed															

Browse numbered routes		
← 74 SR 74	FL	SR 75 75 →
← 74 SR 74	GA	SR 75 75 →
← 74 KY 74	KY	KY 75 75 →
← 74 I-74	OH	I-76 76 →
← 74 M-74	MI	M-75 75 →

Metropolitan Parkway (Detroit area)

Metropolitan Parkway	
Length:	25.23 mi (km)
West end:	[24] US 24 near Bloomfield Hills
Major junctions:	⬥ M-1 in Bloomfield Hills 🅱 I-75 in Troy ⬥ M-53 in Sterling Heights ⬥ M-97 near Mt. Clemens ⬥ M-3 near Mt. Clemens 🅱 I-94 near Mt. Clemens
East end:	Metro Beach Metropark near Mount Clemens

Metropolitan Parkway or **Metro Parkway** is a major thoroughfare in Metro Detroit that stretches west from Metro Beach Metropark. After intersecting several streets, it goes under the names **Big Beaver Road**, **Quarton Road**, and **Walnut Lake Road**. The Metro Parkway name stretches westerly through Macomb County to Dequindre Road, where it crosses into Oakland County and its name changes to Big Beaver Road. Although not technically called such, Metropolitan Parkway corresponds to "16 Mile Road" in Detroit's mile road system and is sometimes referred to that way by area residents, depending on the portion of the road being referred to.

The Big Beaver Corridor Study

In 2006, the Big Beaver Corridor Study was announced, with the goal of making Big Beaver into a world-class boulevard, creating a downtown for Troy, which while having office parks conspicuously lacks a city center (unlike the neighboring towns of Birmingham, Rochester and Royal Oak).

The Big Beaver Corridor Study catalogues, analyzes, and defines issues that will begin a process of planning and directing development opportunities for years to come. Specifically, this document, in part one, provides an overview analysis of existing conditions and summarizes stakeholder and expert opinions as important input for part two efforts to redefine basic and overall corridor characteristics and experience.

Part two addresses the corridor as "world class boulevard" concept, advocated by the DDA as the strategy to re-ignite the development and redevelopment potential of the corridor. Part two outlines specific requirements needed to fulfill this goal. It assigns general land use concepts related to long-term economic viability, transportation management, the urban design aesthetic, and public experience of the corridor.

The study process has resulted in a plan that will fundamentally change the corridor from a traffic-dominant highway to a mixed use urban center, a very dramatic and forward-thinking idea. It also strongly advocates the need for a comprehensive master plan in addition to this study, which will address issues of public and private realm interactions, long-term values, and economic sustainability. This corridor study is an important chapter of that future master plan for the City of Troy.

For more information visit The Big Beaver Corridor Study Website [1].

Notes

- Big Beaver stretches between Dequindre Road and Woodward Avenue (M-1)
- Quarton Road stretches between Woodward and Inkster Road. It is cut off by Gilbert Lake and overlaps Telegraph Road (US 24).
- Walnut Lake Road briefly overlaps Quarton Road but is off track for only one mile and stretches from Franklin Road to Haggerty Road and is discontiguous at some portions.
- Michigan's famous Somerset Collection is located on Big Beaver Road.

Expressway portion

Metro Parkway is an expressway between Schoenherr Road and its eastern terminus. There are no grade separations, however there are at-grade intersections with a notable exception of the grade-separated I-94 interchange. On that stretch, private access is nearly eliminated.

Article Sources and Contributors

Michigan *Source*: http://en.wikipedia.org/?oldid=390673209 *Contributors*: JohnInDC

History of Michigan *Source*: http://en.wikipedia.org/?oldid=386013916 *Contributors*: Allmightyduck

Geography of Michigan *Source*: http://en.wikipedia.org/?oldid=390048243 *Contributors*:

List of Michigan state parks *Source*: http://en.wikipedia.org/?oldid=386373220 *Contributors*: 1 anonymous edits

List of National Historic Landmarks in Michigan *Source*: http://en.wikipedia.org/?oldid=390568986 *Contributors*: Thomas Paine1776

Troy, Michigan *Source*: http://en.wikipedia.org/?oldid=388377769 *Contributors*: Bkonrad

Oakland County, Michigan *Source*: http://en.wikipedia.org/?oldid=388134228 *Contributors*: 1 anonymous edits

Detroit *Source*: http://en.wikipedia.org/?oldid=390620368 *Contributors*: Plastikspork

Metro Detroit *Source*: http://en.wikipedia.org/?oldid=389860682 *Contributors*: Rich Farmbrough

Somerset Collection *Source*: http://en.wikipedia.org/?oldid=383157575 *Contributors*: Thomas Paine1776

Oakland Mall *Source*: http://en.wikipedia.org/?oldid=384721234 *Contributors*: Spears154

Top of Troy *Source*: http://en.wikipedia.org/?oldid=372774321 *Contributors*: Thomas Paine1776

Detroit Red Wings *Source*: http://en.wikipedia.org/?oldid=390063595 *Contributors*:

Transportation in metropolitan Detroit *Source*: http://en.wikipedia.org/?oldid=390370689 *Contributors*: Thomas Paine1776

Big Beaver Airport *Source*: http://en.wikipedia.org/?oldid=333323509 *Contributors*: The Anome

Oakland-Troy Airport *Source*: http://en.wikipedia.org/?oldid=228883739 *Contributors*:

Interstate 75 *Source*: http://en.wikipedia.org/?oldid=387972189 *Contributors*: C.Fred

Metropolitan Parkway (Detroit area) *Source*: http://en.wikipedia.org/?oldid=390220014 *Contributors*:

Image Sources, Licenses and Contributors

File:Flag_of_Michigan.svg *Source*: http://bibliocm.bibliolabs.com/mwAnon/index.php?title=File:Flag_of_Michigan.svg *License*: unknown *Contributors*: Awg1010, Denelson83, Dzordzm, Fry1989, Homo lupus, Mattes, Serinde, Svgalbertian, Werewombat, 1 anonymous edits

File:Seal of Michigan.svg *Source*: http://bibliocm.bibliolabs.com/mwAnon/index.php?title=File:Seal_of_Michigan.svg *License*: unknown *Contributors*: Designed by Lewis Cass

File:Map_of_USA_MI.svg *Source*: http://bibliocm.bibliolabs.com/mwAnon/index.php?title=File:Map_of_USA_MI.svg *License*: Creative Commons Attribution 2.0 *Contributors*: Abnormaal, Hogweard, Huebi, Lokal Profil, Lupo, Mattbuck, Petr Dlouhý, 2 anonymous edits

File:Michigan 1718.jpg *Source*: http://bibliocm.bibliolabs.com/mwAnon/index.php?title=File:Michigan_1718.jpg *License*: Public Domain *Contributors*: Original uploader was Billwhittaker at en.wikipedia

File:Hauling at Thomas Foster's, by Jenney, J A (detail).jpg *Source*: http://bibliocm.bibliolabs.com/mwAnon/index.php?title=File:Hauling_at_Thomas_Foster's,_by_Jenney,_J_A_(detail).jpg *License*: unknown *Contributors*: Rmhermen

File:Granholm speaking to troops, Lansing, 1 Dec, 2005.jpg *Source*: http://bibliocm.bibliolabs.com/mwAnon/index.php?title=File:Granholm_speaking_to_troops,_Lansing,_1_Dec,_2005.jpg *License*: Public Domain *Contributors*: SFC Jim Dowen, Jr.

File:Sleeping Bear Dune Aerial View.jpg *Source*: http://bibliocm.bibliolabs.com/mwAnon/index.php?title=File:Sleeping_Bear_Dune_Aerial_View.jpg *License*: Public Domain *Contributors*: National Park Service employee

File:Tahquamenon falls upper.jpg *Source*: http://bibliocm.bibliolabs.com/mwAnon/index.php?title=File:Tahquamenon_falls_upper.jpg *License*: Creative Commons Attribution 2.5 *Contributors*: User:anagy

File:Pointe Mouillee.jpg *Source*: http://bibliocm.bibliolabs.com/mwAnon/index.php?title=File:Pointe_Mouillee.jpg *License*: Public Domain *Contributors*: U.S. Army Corps of Engineers, photographer not specified or unknown

File:Little Sable Light Point Light Station - Michigan.jpg *Source*: http://bibliocm.bibliolabs.com/mwAnon/index.php?title=File:Little_Sable_Light_Point_Light_Station_-_Michigan.jpg *License*: Creative Commons Attribution 2.5 *Contributors*: Jjegers at en.wikipedia

File:Michigan.svg *Source*: http://bibliocm.bibliolabs.com/mwAnon/index.php?title=File:Michigan.svg *License*: GNU Free Documentation License *Contributors*: Phizzy (talk).

File:MichiganHardinessZones.svg *Source*: http://bibliocm.bibliolabs.com/mwAnon/index.php?title=File:MichiganHardinessZones.svg *License*: GNU Free Documentation License *Contributors*: Phizzy (talk).

File:Michigan population map.png *Source*: http://bibliocm.bibliolabs.com/mwAnon/index.php?title=File:Michigan_population_map.png *License*: GNU Free Documentation License *Contributors*: Original uploader was JimIrwin at en.wikipedia

File:MichiganAncestry.svg *Source*: http://bibliocm.bibliolabs.com/mwAnon/index.php?title=File:MichiganAncestry.svg *License*: GNU Free Documentation License *Contributors*: Phizzy (talk). Original uploader was Phizzy at en.wikipedia

File:Michigan Cherries, 2009 July.jpg *Source*: http://bibliocm.bibliolabs.com/mwAnon/index.php?title=File:Michigan_Cherries,_2009_July.jpg *License*: Creative Commons Attribution 2.0 *Contributors*: Steven Depolo

File:Grand Hotel-Mackinac Island.jpg *Source*: http://bibliocm.bibliolabs.com/mwAnon/index.php?title=File:Grand_Hotel-Mackinac_Island.jpg *License*: Attribution *Contributors*: David Ball

File:Mackinac Bridge Sunset.jpg *Source*: http://bibliocm.bibliolabs.com/mwAnon/index.php?title=File:Mackinac_Bridge_Sunset.jpg *License*: Creative Commons Attribution 3.0 *Contributors*: User:Dehk

File:Michigan entrance sign.JPG *Source*: http://bibliocm.bibliolabs.com/mwAnon/index.php?title=File:Michigan_entrance_sign.JPG *License*: Public Domain *Contributors*: User:Lovemykia

File:Grskyline2.jpg *Source*: http://bibliocm.bibliolabs.com/mwAnon/index.php?title=File:Grskyline2.jpg *License*: Public Domain *Contributors*: User:Bhyse23

File:1 Lansing Pan.jpg *Source*: http://bibliocm.bibliolabs.com/mwAnon/index.php?title=File:1_Lansing_Pan.jpg *License*: GNU Free Documentation License *Contributors*: User Criticalthinker on en.wikipedia

File:Flint skyline2.jpg *Source*: http://bibliocm.bibliolabs.com/mwAnon/index.php?title=File:Flint_skyline2.jpg *License*: Public Domain *Contributors*: Xnatedawgx, Yassie

File:DownTownAA1 copy.jpg *Source*: http://bibliocm.bibliolabs.com/mwAnon/index.php?title=File:DownTownAA1_copy.jpg *License*: Creative Commons Attribution 3.0 *Contributors*: Alan Piracha (Alanmi88)

File:MichiganCities.svg *Source*: http://bibliocm.bibliolabs.com/mwAnon/index.php?title=File:MichiganCities.svg *License*: GNU Free Documentation License *Contributors*: Phizzy (talk).

File:Flag of Japan.svg *Source*: http://bibliocm.bibliolabs.com/mwAnon/index.php?title=File:Flag_of_Japan.svg *License*: Public Domain *Contributors*: Various

File:Flag of the People's Republic of China.svg *Source*: http://bibliocm.bibliolabs.com/mwAnon/index.php?title=File:Flag_of_the_People's_Republic_of_China.svg *License*: Public Domain *Contributors*: User:Denelson83, User:SKopp, User:Shizhao, User:Zscout370

Image:Soo Locks-Sault-Ste Marie.png *Source*: http://bibliocm.bibliolabs.com/mwAnon/index.php?title=File:Soo_Locks-Sault-Ste_Marie.png *License*: Public Domain *Contributors*: AnRo0002, Appraiser, Feydey, Geofrog, Jkelly, Juiced lemon, Kimdime, Mattes, Mircea, Rmhermen, Xnatedawgx, Yassie, 5 anonymous edits

Image:Last glacial vegetation map.png *Source*: http://bibliocm.bibliolabs.com/mwAnon/index.php?title=File:Last_glacial_vegetation_map.png *License*: unknown *Contributors*: Ciaurlec, DieBuche, Fabartus, Glenn, Innotata, JMCC1, Joey-das-WBF, Jrockley, MaxEnt, Mmcannis, Santosga, SchuminWeb, Slomox, 4 anonymous edits

Image:Michigan 1718.jpg *Source*: http://bibliocm.bibliolabs.com/mwAnon/index.php?title=File:Michigan_1718.jpg *License*: Public Domain *Contributors*: Original uploader was Billwhittaker at en.wikipedia

Image:Treaty of Paris by Benjamin West 1783.jpg *Source*: http://bibliocm.bibliolabs.com/mwAnon/index.php?title=File:Treaty_of_Paris_by_Benjamin_West_1783.jpg *License*: Public Domain *Contributors*: Bogdan, Clindberg, Daderot, Jkllee, Man vyi, Nonenmac, Shakko, The Red Hat of Pat Ferrick

Image:Flint Sit-Down Strike window.jpg *Source*: http://bibliocm.bibliolabs.com/mwAnon/index.php?title=File:Flint_Sit-Down_Strike_window.jpg *License*: unknown *Contributors*: Sheldon Dick

CPSIA information can be obtained at www.ICGtesting.com
Printed in the USA
BVOW10s0610270415

397826BV00006BB/40/P